The Unfolding Self

The Unfolding Self
Separation and Individuation

Mara Sidoli

SIGO Press
Boston

SIGO Press
25 New Chardon Street, #8748
Boston, Massachusetts 02114

Publisher and General Editor: Sisa Sternback

ISBN 0-938434-66-7 (cloth) $29.95
ISBN 0-938434-65-9 (pbk.) $15.95

Library of Congress Cataloging-in-Publication Data

Sidoli, Mara
    The unfolding self: separation and individuation/ Mara Sidoli
    p. cm.   Includes bibliographical references
    1. Self. 2. Separation-individuation. 3. Psychology,
Pathological. 4. Psychotherapy. I. Title
    [DNLM: 1. Personality Development. 2. Self Concept. BF
    698   S569u]
RC455.4.S42S54 1989
618.92'89 – dc20
DNLM/DLC
for Library of Congress   89-10739
                                                          CIP

Shape clay into a vessel
It is the shape within
that makes it useful.
           Lao-tsu
           From the *Tao Te Ching*
           Jane English, trans.

Table of Contents

PREFACE

It gives me much pleasure to write something by way of introduction to Mara Sidoli's book. When in the late 1930's I started to become interested in the psychotherapy of children. I was the only Jungian to believe in the importance of that discipline. It was currently held that a child's ego was so weak that it was not possible to analyze him. Consequently, as his emotional life was so much bound up with his parents, it must be they who needed treatment if their child showed behavioral or neurotic characteristics. Once their noxious effect had been withdrawn all would be well with their child.

Today, the picture in analytical psychology is vastly different so that analysis and psychotherapy with children is widely recognized as an effective and valuable discipline. The impetus for this change undoubtedly emanated from the Society of Analytical Psychology in London where a small group of analysts persued their interest in childhood. Eventually, a training in child analysis was instituted and Mara Sidoli was among the first of our trainees. She has since participated in the training, especially by organizing seminars on mother/infant observations. It was with much regret and a sense of loss to us in England that she has moved her center of operation to Santa Fe in New Mexico.

Her new book, following on *Jungian Child Psychotherapy*, which she edited in collaboration with Miranda Davies, marks a milestone in the literature of analytical psychology. It draws together work with children and adult patients showing in vivid description how a knowledge of children and infancy can enrich a Jungian analysis of all age groups. That is done with great skill: she does not depart into abstract theorizing but uses theory only as a framework for her entrancing descriptions. How she works with child and adult patients is thus beautifully displayed so that the book is not only technically important but also eminently readable.

                                        Michael Fordham
                                        Jordans, September, 1989

FOREWORD

People and personal relationships have always been of paramount importance in my life, but my on-going interest in infants and children, and how adults do or do not relate to them, was the factor which motivated me in becoming an analyst; this book is thus the result of many years of work in clinical practice with patients of all ages.

I have always been aware of how much of the child adults carry around within themselves, though most of the time they are unaware of the fact, denying it, believing themselves to be fully "grown up." Yet it is important that the real child, as well as the child within, be acknowledged and understood, especially in the analytic interaction, because it is from this "internal child" that emotional energy and vitality originate.

This is a central concept in the analysis of children and adults alike. To be able to engage and support this child part of the patient, while at the same time keeping it in check, to allow for space, and to make oneself emotionally available to allow for an affective interplay within that space, all of this means letting the child develop, grow, and feel free about expressing him or herself. This in turn will enrich the patient's experience of him or herself within the analytic space, while work on the transference-countertransference will offer a potential for the integration of neglected aspects of the personality—which takes place because, through the transference, past relationships can be safely reenacted in the present. With the analyst's help and empathic understanding, the patient can develop a greater capacity to tolerate and profit from his or her own weaknesses.

In terms of the theoretical foundations of this book, I am very fortunate to have had the opportunity to train in London with the Society of Analytical Psychology and Dr. Michael Fordham, whose ideas and theoretical approach to training and analysis attracted me from the start. Following my personal interest, I started by training as a child analyst, training which at the time was available only in London at the S.A.P. The child analytical training provided the opportunity to integrate the more traditional Jungian approach with infant-observation and child-development seminars, as well as to be exposed to the Kleinian and Freudian theory and praxis of working with children in analysis. This invaluable experience has allowed me to integrate the various schools of thought currently operating in the field of child analysis.

I was immediately attracted by the potential of infant observation and infant research as a unique means of empirically validating Jung's theories about the self and the archetypes. The unfolding of the Primal Self (Fordham) through deintegration-reintegration, for instance, could be verified by observation; far from being a completely abstract construct, it struck me as a very specific developmental phenomenon, something I have been able to observe in real infants as well as in the internal "infant" of the patient in analysis.

I would like to express my gratitude to Dorothy Davidson and to the late Jess Guthrie for the support and help they gave me in their roles of supervisor in child-analysis training. Above all, they helped me persevere and endure the hardships of training, and they honed my empathic and analytic capacity. My subsequent training as an adult analyst allowed me to acquire a more balanced view of the relationship between the adult and the child, exposed me to the Jungian world of archetypal images and to object-relations theories, and allowed me to appreciate the teaching of many brilliant seminar leaders. I have been greatly influenced by my supervisor Dr. Kenneth Lambert, whose original, personal, and humane approach to the patient has left a permanent stamp on my analytic style. Special thanks go to my colleague Miranda Davies for her patience in helping me revise and edit this book. I would also like to thank my husband and my children for having supported my work and enriched my personal life. Finally, I would like to thank all my patients, who made this book possible by sharing with me the accounts of their lives.

Mara Sidoli
Santa Fe, NM
June 1989

The Unfolding Self

Chapter 1

THE SELF IN INFANCY AND CHILDHOOD

Separation is essentially paradoxical. In my view the experience of separation is needed in order to form sufficient ego strength to achieve this end. (Ruth Strauss, 1962)

Jung did not formulate a theory of child development, but rather of the development of consciousness out of the unconscious, a process through which, according to him, "a person becomes a psychological individual, that is, a separate indivisible unit or 'whole'" (Jung, 1939).

On the whole, he viewed the first part of life, from birth to puberty, as being dominated by instinctuality. He believed that ego growth and adaptation take place in childhood, whereas individuation proper begins in adult life. He writes: "The child is as if he were not yet completely born but were still enclosed in the psychic atmosphere of his parents." To Jung, psychic birth meant "conscious differentiation from the parents [such as] would normally take place in adolescence with the eruption of sexuality" (Jung, "The stages of life," 1930/31). His studies on myths and dreams and his observations of archetypal imagery of the self in the material brought to him by his adult patients focused

1

mainly on the second half of life.

The Self:
The Ego and the Archetypes

Jung conceived of the self as the totality of the psyche, combining conscious with unconscious and containing ego and archetypes. He derived this concept from his studies of oriental religions and mysticism, and from his lived experience. However, he also viewed the self as the archetype of order. This then expresses the self's paradoxical nature.

The archetypes were conceived of by Jung as the organizers of experience, which operate within the self in the service of the ego. "There are innate predispositions which although not characterised by the quality of experience which we call consciousness, none the less determine and structure the relationship between the internal and external world" (Jung, 1939*). His interest in a multitude of complex studies led him away from specific research on childhood, but he mentioned that he had found in children's drawings and dreams "self-symbols" (such as rudimentary representations of mandalas or circles) like those he had discovered in the material brought by adult patients.

Among Jung's contemporaries, Frances Wickes became interested in working with children, but she did not leave a systematic account of her approach to child psychotherapy. She followed Jung's views that children are mainly influenced by the unconscious of the parents.

Michael Fordham was the British analyst who innovatively applied Jung's theoretical concepts to childhood and infancy. From Jung's concept of the self Fordham derived the "primal self," which, in his view, represents the totality of psyche and soma

---

*Note: The archetype in itself is not knowable, but it manifests itself in typical imagery which has archetypal characteristics. The archetypes most commonly constellated are, according to Jung: the Ego, the persona, the shadow, the mother, the father, the child, and the anima and the animus. All have a positive and negative side. Jung wrote: "There are as many archetypes as there are typical situations in life" (1959).

in a germinal state from the very start of intrauterine life. The primal self is conceptualized as a "steady state of integration" from which the child's ego and bodily growth will unfold through dynamic processes he termed "deintegration-reintegration" (Fordham, 1976).

According to Jung's definition, archetypal activity is located within the self. Jung defined archetypes as mental representations of instincts and/or innate predispositions to experience life according to certain patterns. If we assume that they become operative at the onset of life, during the course of the first deintegration of the primal self after birth, the affects and instincts of which the archetypes are "mental representations" are "collective"—that is, common to all human beings. With regard to this, Michael Fordham writes:

> By conceiving archetypes as dynamic structures closely related to drives, expressed in impulses originating in neurophysiological structures and biochemical changes, the theory of archetypes brings body and psyche together and makes Jung's thesis as to their bipolarity particularly meaningful: the archetypes are unconscious entities having two poles, the one expressing itself in instinctual impulses and drives, the other in spiritual forms. In contrast to the instinctual drives, which are relatively fixed and few in number, the spiritual component has wide and flexible application. Transferring this idea to childhood and starting from the spiritual components, the theory of archetypes means that a predisposition exists in the child to develop archaic ideas, feelings and fantasies without their being implanted in him or without his introjecting them. These can be influenced and refined by education which in turn, as in feedback systems, provide suitable imagery through which the unconscious archetypes can find expression in consciousness. It is on the spiritual pole that parents build when they mediate the culture pattern of the society in which the developing organism is living. (Fordham, 1976 p. 5)

In early infancy, when neurophysiological drives and discharges prevail, oral, anal, and urethral impulses provide the ground-roots for archetypal imagery of a primitive and violent character later on in life. In infancy, however, we can infer the existence of proto-images, such as shapes and patterns, in the baby's mind, which, enriched by sensuous experiences, will in time develop into proper images of objects and people.

Jung's *Psychology of the Transference* (1954) illustrates his theory of mental functioning in relation to instinctual discharges. He writes:

> The instincts and their specific fantasy-contents are partly concrete, partly symbolical (i.e., "unreal"), sometimes one, sometimes the other. . . . We know that it is possible to interpret the fantasy-contents of the instincts either as *signs*, as self-portraits of the instincts, i.e., reductively; or as *symbols*, as the spiritual meaning of the natural instinct. In the former case the instinctive process is taken to be "real" and in the latter "unreal." (p. 175)

Here Jung refers to the bipolarity of the archetype.

In the early stages of life we have to take into account primarily the "bodily pole" of the archetype. Its symbolic and spiritual polarity, although potentially present, is not yet available to the infant, who is immersed in sensuous experiences of a subjective and undifferentiated kind, a stage where impulses predominate. For instance, early cannibalistic oral impulses toward the breast give rise to unconscious fantasies of devouring or being devoured, which the child will express later on by projecting them onto gobbling mouths, devouring teeth, biting monsters, and beasts with fangs and big teeth, as these images become available to him through the influence of the environment.

Bowlby (1973) points out that the fear of predators in children who have suffered traumatic geographical separation from their mothers in their early years is more acute than that in children who, by the presence of the real mother, have been sheltered from extreme persecutory experiences at the oral sadistic stage (while teething). In other words, the latter have often been protected from the impact of unanticipated archetypal experiences of oral sadism — in infancy instinctual needs have a special urgency, and this urge is expressed by the baby through fits of screaming, panic, and other kinds of affect-loaded somatizations. The infant has as yet no means of representing them symbolically and no actual language with which to communicate. This applies to all instinctual needs in infantile urethral and anal impulses which may give rise to anxiety states connected with the fear of annihilation, or of one's own body—or the maternal one—exploding or melting away. In childhood and in later life such unconscious anxiety states come to be represented in play or dream material by volcanic explosions, bombing, earthquakes, fires, drowning, floods and so on. The satisfaction of the early and violent and instinctual urges produces in turn states of total well-being, which at the time are expressed by the buddha-like drowsy states of infants who, after a good feed, drop gently into sleep. These states and feelings give rise to a sense of peace, harmony, beauty, and joy, which later on in life can find expression both in creative imagery and in relationships.

In infancy the activity of the primal self is intense and structured according to deintegration-reintegration processes, whereas ego consciousness is discontinuous and unstructured. Given such situations, one can infer that an infant tends to experience the absolute dimension of the archetypes.

According to Fordham's theory, ego fragments—that is to say, "deintegrates and the primal self"—are at the mercy of deintegrative-reintegrative sequences during the course of the painful process of ego growth and adaptation to life. Swings in affect suddenly raise or lower danger signals for the infant. Threats of disintegration as well as experiences of unintegrated and incoherent states constitute a large part of this stage of life.

Because the dynamic systems of the self act as disturbances that run counter to the nascent ego's need to coalesce, infants deal with experiences according to whether they feel "good" or "bad." In this way the innate predisposition for human experience is organized according to patterns (archetypes) that recreate extreme collective contents in the individual human being.

Many writers have tried to express in words or images these very early experiences of goodness and badness. In his own way, Jung adopted the concept of the archetypes and derived a multitude of archetypal images of both goodness and evil from myths and fairy tales. Winnifred Bion conceptualized it as "thinking the unthinkable." Donald Meltzer describes the experience of goodness in infancy as being overwhelmed by the beauty of the breast. In my view, these are all attempts by adults to put into words and concepts the extreme early experiences of total bliss and fulfillment, as well as panic, dread, and unthinkable violence. These states are unthinkable because they are experienced in the preverbal and preconceptual stage of human life, when subject and object are not yet perceived as differentiated, so that the experience has an all-encompassing feel to it.

Fordham's Theory of the Primal Self

When the primal self (a steady state) deintegrates, it allows for the dynamic systems (observable soon after birth) to begin to work (Fordham, 1976). The psychic energy bound up in the primal integrate divides into opposites, constellating the opposing archetypal experiences, which are psychophysiological in nature. Thus the child's ego unfolds and shapes itself through deintegrative-reintegrative processes from the primal self. Individuating processes are, in fact, operative from a very early age.

Fordham has often stressed that in intrauterine life and after birth an infant is separate from his mother and is a psychological being in his own right. Recent ultrasound scans on foetuses in the womb provide increasing evidence that from the very beginning each foetus has its own individuality (Piontelli, 1987). Thus Michael Fordham's hypothesis of the individuality of the infant is now actually observable. He conceptualizes the primal self as the original state of wholeness. According to him, in the early stages of life the infant "is mainly unconscious but not totally unconscious," often — but not always — in an integrated state, a state of identity. Thus states of identity with the self and states of awareness of separateness seem to coexist and alternate from the very beginning, the former having, at first, prevailed together with a capacity to know about the mother's emotional state and mothering abilities. These processes take place within the "nursing couple activities and presuppose sufficiently good parenting to be facilitated." (Fordham, 1969)

The Mother's Function in the Nursing Couple

The presence of the mother is of the utmost importance in this phase. Her psychological task is to intervene and support her infant's ego (as yet fragmentary) with her own ego, just as with her physical care she looks after and attends to her baby's needs. Thus she metabolizes and transforms into thoughts and ideas, and gives a name to, those archetypal experiences that the baby is living through. All this can take place as the energy released in deintegration produces instability and tension, which drive the infant toward the outer world (breast/mother) in order to release the tension.

In the first stage of life differentiation is minimal; the infant's experience is very limited, but it is acquired within the interaction with the mother and the emergence of consciousness and ego structuring. Thus the importance of primary maternal care and preoccupation is self-evident, and one can also witness the degree of empathy required in a mother to facilitate her baby's difficult life task.

All being well during the first two years of life, the baby will manage to incarnate the terrifying archetypal parental images into the real flesh-and-blood parents; the parents in turn will channel him towards experiencing and sustaining limitations and frustrations to his omnipotent wishes and fantasies derived from archetypal activity. Thus the limitations and frustrations imposed by reality will support and promote ego growth and the acquisition of the child's own areas of competence by decreasing the feelings of helplessness that tend to give rise to fantasies of omnipotence.

On the other hand, the baby can also not be considered as impotent. He has available—and seems to be well aware of—the means by which he can elicit strong responses in the mother—crying and screaming, cooing and smiling—which normally bring about her intervention. The baby's capacity (or lack of it) to elicit a response from his mother and to relate to her, independently of the mother's empathy and degree of capacity to relate to the baby, has been pointed out by Fordham and has also been observed in infant observation studies, confirming the validity and usefulness of this theoretical approach to infancy and childhood.

Deintegration in the Mother

Giving birth is a major emotional as well as physical experience for a woman. In order for it to be integrated, the mother's self/ego axis undergoes a major deintegration. This, in turn, predisposes her to regress in order to get in touch with the infantile layers of her personality, which will help her to empathize with her newborn.

This process, of course, unsettles the maternal ego. In a normal situation—that is to say, when a *dis*integration does not take place in the mother—a reintegration follows, fairly smoothly reestablishing the ego balance. However, when disintegration occurs, a post-partum psychosis or depression may take place. The birth event is also disruptive of the relationship in the couple. Just as the woman has to deintegrate to become a mother, so the husband has to deintegrate to become a father. This creates a regressive state in the couple, which, together with the physical demands of the real baby, gives rise for the first months after a birth to a very delicate situation in the family, which will often need much external support to carry on functioning (where grandparents, health visitors, and so on come in very handy). Usually the situation improves once the reef of the third month is overcome by the baby and the whole family.

Separation in Space and Time

Returning to the definition by Jung that individuation denotes a process by which a person becomes a psychological individual — that is to say, a separate indivisible unit — it must be stressed that although at birth a baby is a separate unit from the mother, the baby psychologically does not experience this separation, so long as he feels integrated.

However, the integrated state represents only one aspect of the dynamic system that sets to work at birth, and it also alternates with deintegrated states. During deintegrated states the search for the breast (mother) begins to be experienced as something distinct and not arising from inside the primal self. It is presented physically by the baby opening his mouth, turning his head sideways with slobbering lips, making sucking noises, crying, and eventually bringing his thumb to his mouth as a comforter if the breast cannot be found.

Frances Tustin suggests that "in early infantile development there is an awareness of separatedness which is made tolerable in the baby by auto-sensuous activities and bodily interactions with other people, especially mother" (Tustin, 1986). Here Tustin is describing attempts on the part of the baby to bring about a reintegration.

It is in the course of the deintegrative phase, while waiting for the breast to appear and the nipple to fill the open painful gap in the mouth, but not knowing for certain that this will happen, that the maximal survival panic and the precursor of separation anxiety are experienced — the degree of intensity varying according to the span of the excessive waiting. It is also during the deintegrative phase, prolonged beyond what is bearable to the infant and his individual needs in that specific stage of his development, that disintegration may be experienced.

Disintegration in infancy takes the form of screaming, becoming red in the face, breathlessness, vomiting, shaking, wetting, and defecating in a crescendo, all at the same time, as if an explosion had taken place. Consequently the baby will be unable to take the nipple back in the mouth and use the comfort provided by the mother for a very long time, as I have observed. The length of time seems to vary in accordance with the duration of the preceding frustrated expectation.

Initially, in the very first days of life, being thrown from a relatively peaceful state in the womb ("relatively" because a great many activities go on in the uterus) into a completely alien environment, the full swing of the deintegrative processes of the self/ego axis dynamism tends to create a state of panic and shock to the infant, which he can just manage with the constant support of his mother. Having his needs not met instantly creates a gap, a sense of frustrating absence. The capacity to tolerate the open gap — an amount which varies from baby to baby — is slowly developed with the help of the mother and of autoerotic activities such as thumb sucking, and with the experience of deintegration being followed by reintegration time after time.

The feeling of being separate from the mother and being able to survive increases with the building up of trust that the breast, which goes away, keeps coming back. In this way the baby can accept dependency and be confident while waiting. When things do not go smoothly, the baby experiences being too exposed during the deintegrative phase of development and tends to use defensive mechanisms, called by Fordham "defences of the self," to avoid falling into a disintegration.

The dream of an adult patient in the seventh month of his analysis demonstrates how these defences operate through images. This is important because the images in the dream illustrate, in adult language, the states of undifferentiated being experienced by babies who as yet are in an imageless state. The baby's experience is thus expressed psychosomatically. This man, in his early thirties, had a serious problem with relationships, which came about from his early misconnection with his mother. The mother's own inner child was deprived and immature, which prevented her from tuning in to her baby's needs and made her either impinge on his vital areas or leave him unattended for too long.

Defences of the self, as Fordham describes, are set in motion in the baby's self in order to protect his vulnerable parts. In analysis, this patient fiercely resisted lying on the couch. The dream that I shall report here occurred about a week after he had gone on the couch, where he lay almost immobile and curled up. It was reported by him with complaints of great anguish and feelings of constraint. It was observable from his physical posture that in the transference his baby self experienced me as a dangerous and unpredictable enemy:

> I am very small, a baby. I am in a leather bag that envelops me but it seems not to cover my legs and feet, so I curl them up to keep them inside. All around there are objects like feet, claws and teeth, which try to get at me. I am safe if the bag is closed, but the bag has a kind of autonomous mechanism by which, like a zipper, it opens and closes rhythmically, exposing my belly and my front parts. I feel very vulnerable, panicky and in danger; then I realise that I can use my arms, which are hard like a winged shield, to pull in front to cover the opening and protect myself from the vicious attack of those awful claws.

His attempts in the dream — by curling up and returning to a closed-up foetal position — to stop the bag opening and exposing his soft vulnerable parts to attacks from bad persecuting objects seem to serve the purpose of keeping him inside the womb in a safer and imaginary state of oneness with, and inside, the mother. He seems to be fighting with all his capacity the deintegrative process of the primal self. So far as his life experience goes, this is a man whose actual birth took 48 hours; but when referring to it his mother seemed unaware of her baby's sufferings.

The theory of the primal self is useful to describe babies in the first weeks after birth, when they are mostly within the self in an integrated state (i.e. asleep), as they were before birth, except when the drive discharges as hunger, pain, discomfort, and so on, making the self deintegrate and the baby begin to root, searching for the breast.

During states of wakefulness and alertness, which are less frequent at this stage of life, minor adjustments are constantly taking place, but these are less charged with affects. Because deintegration and reintegration follow rhythmic sequences, the concept of time is implicit in this theory, and everything can go smoothly as long as there is syntony or resonance between the deintegrating of the primal self and the archetypal expectations that are met by the object—the mother.

Frances Tustin describes the early infantile experiences of the baby-mother dyad in the following way:

> In early infancy the infant's lack of discrimination, and the mother's adaptation arising from empathic identification with him in the form of "reverie" (Bion, 1962a, p. 309), serve to minimize the explosion-producing gap between primitive illusion and actuality. This empathic reciprocity at first fosters the illusion of bodily continuity, and then gradually acclimatizes the nursing couple to the dimly apprehended fact of separateness. It enables the mother to support her infant through the turbulence arising from awareness of separateness; separateness which seems to be experienced as a break in bodily continuity—a loss of a part of a body.

According to Tustin, this also tends to happen in the adequate nursing situation, but,

> A mother with unbearable, unformulated infantile insecurities, and little support in bearing them, finds it difficult to take such projections from her infant. In a way, both mother and child are too alike in their reactions. Such a mother easily succumbs to attacks on her capacity to pay attention to her infant—to hold him in her awareness. Such attacks may come from her own infantile "privations," or from outside events and people, or from her infant's atmospheric reactions; it is usually a combination of these. They mean that her attention is gone,

her mind wanders. . . . It seems that the mother, through no
fault of her own, is absent-minded, the "holding situation"
(Winnicott, 1958, p. 268) is broken. (Tustin, 1986)

In the early phases, the baby will have the illusion of being
at one with the breast—that is, of having the breast inside, or
of having "created the breast," as Winnicot puts it. Once this
phase is properly established, separation can begin to be
tolerated.

However, when the breast does not appear to fit the expectation, then the baby has to endure the frustrating awareness that
something is missing, that "it" may not be available and may not
be part of the totality that it perceived as "himself," i.e. the whole
world. (The finding of the breast, or the union of mouth and
nipple, allows for a new reintegration to take place, thus filling
up the frustrating time gaps). In those cases when deintegration occurs and the archetypal expectations are not met (mouth-
nipple, the need to be held, holding arms and so on) the reintegration that follows takes place not on the basis of an experience in flesh and blood, but on the basis of the constellation
in the infant's psyche of an archetypal image of the great mother breast (or hallucination of the breast, in Freudian terms).

The archetypal images of the breast not mediated by the real
mother seem to grip the baby, who, while sucking his own thumb,
will relate to an archetypal representation of sucking (deintegration of sucking) the breast, and will feel that the actual nipple
is filling up the empty frustrating gap in his mouth. So far all
will be well, because in this way he will avoid a disintegration,
managing to survive until the real mother returns. However, if
the archetypal deintegrate "baby-sits" for the mother too often—
that is, if the baby is left to hold himself together by himself
for too long—no growth can occur because autistic defences
(defences of the self) come into play, preventing a relationship
to the real mother from taking place, as in the case of the patient
mentioned above.

Babies Observed

There are, however, babies who by reason of an innate fragility cannot at first tolerate the slightest gap between the need for the breast and the fulfilment of that need. For these babies no amount of maternal syntonic empathy seems to be sufficient.

Infant observation research notes that certain babies are more alert and outward-looking soon after birth than others. This seems to have to do both with their innate liveliness and with making an immediate good "fit" with a "mother-world" geared to accommodate them, and with as much sense of being at one as possible, and good personal resources, hence with the least possible experience of gaps and traumas. Other babies, however, appear to arrive in life as "not quite born" and take a long time to open themselves to it. Some babies are born while sound asleep (Prechtel, 1973). This state of affairs seems to be reinforced by a premature sense of separateness and hostility, mixed with anxiety, on the part of the mother about the baby keeping to itself and appearing not to need her. Such a situation usually results in a bad "fit" and, occasionally, in a "nonfit," with tragic consequences for the baby and terrible anxieties, guilt, and frustration in the mother.

The following is an example of a baby girl who took a long time to wake up into life. She appears to fit the description of Prechtel's baby—born while asleep.

From the beginning, Kay showed a specific difficulty with deintegrative-reintegrative dynamics. She was born two weeks early and exhibited difficulties in coming out of the primal self, in Fordham's terms. It was noted in the seminars that she did not show much expectation for interacting with the breast during the first weeks of her life. A few extracts from the observations show this clearly happening after an eleven-week period. The observations were recorded by Diana Campi, who has kindly allowed me to quote from them.

Kay was born at 8:30 a.m., after an easy birth. The mother

did not welcome her appearance, and she was taken away to be cleaned up. She was returned to the mother at 4 p.m., and the mother attempted to put her to the breast, but this was not successful, and she did not respond to the nipple. During the first days after birth the mother described her as having difficulty in finding the nipple but "a gobbler" once the breast was in her mouth. She did not cry for the first 48 hours after birth, and at the end of the second day only because she passed so many stools that she needed bathing, and then she only cried during diaper changing. The mother expressed anxiety about Kay and enquired if all was right with her.

During both the first and the second visits Kay was sound asleep, not stirring for the whole of the observation, either in the crib at the foot of the mother's bed, or held, the second time, on the father's lap.

The mother was distant and too anxious and shocked by the birth to be able to relate to Kay. She was a woman of 40 who had wanted a baby for a long time but became pregnant only after she had given up all hope of ever having a baby. Her bewilderment and shock were understandable, but the hospital practice of removing the baby from the mother for such a long period of time did not help the bonding process for this nursing couple, as the distance between mother and baby was too great for too long. Kay, following the first deintegration at birth, appears to have reverted quickly back into the primal self—as if locking herself up in it—in order to avoid the dread of disintegration in her premature isolation. As a consequence, this state of affairs gives rise to a difficulty in deintegration: she cannot find the nipple, does not cry or evacuate for two whole days, and sleeps all the time, holding her fists clenched and her mouth tightly closed. One may hypothesize that she slept through her birth as I pointed out earlier.

In his book, *Psychoanalysis and Infant Research,* Lichtenberg stresses that "Attachment is based on mutual reciprocity. Infants almost immediately demonstrate an expectancy for engagement in their rhythmic cycling of attention and nonattention. . . . 'The precision of synchronisation is so striking in many of these interactions that the researchers emphasise participation within organisation forms rather than viewing each partner's contribution as discrete and separate' (Condon and Sanders, 1974)." These findings led researchers to conclude that, "Mothering behaviour is primed for the immediate postpartum period" and that "early separation can adversely affect the developing maternal attachment bond" (Barnett, 1970; Peterson, 1978; Mehl, 1978).

These findings provide evidence for the theory of cyclic and rhythmic processes in the self of both mothers and babies, of opening up and closing down, searching for the other and turning back inside. Deintegration-reintegration takes place in both, and if the tuning-in on the part of the mother is delayed by the early removal of the baby, which occurs in many hospitals, the bonding may be much more difficult and, at times, impossible.

> Kay was ten days old when the observer arrived, and she was asleep and had to be woken up by the mother to be fed. Although the mother said it was feeding time, Kay did not wake up, even when she was picked up and brought downstairs. The mother talked to the observer, but Kay did not seem to react. The mother then sat down in an armchair and, making herself comfortable, prepared to feed Kay. Laying her on her left side in her right arm, she gently put the nipple to her mouth. The baby fussed for a while, not taking the nipple straight away, and then suddenly found it. "She takes a little while to get started," said the mother, "then she lunges at me. She is a real guzzler. She usually feeds for around fifteen minutes and then has a doze, so I change her before putting her to the other breast." The mother suddenly let out a cry and said that Kay had latched herself so firmly on to her breast at the beginning that it hurt. Kay lay in the mother's arms, both hands still encased by the all-in-one suit lying across her chest and under her chin. She was quite motionless except for the strong sound of sucking. The mother now stopped her and sat her up for a moment. Kay's eyes were half open; she vomited, and her mother gently cleaned her on top of her head, picked her up and put her over her shoulder and walked toward the door saying she would change her.
>
> The observer followed her back into the sitting room and sat down again. The mother prepared herself again to feed

Kay and gently held out her left nipple. This time Kay took it straight away, with one arm straight out in front and the other held in the air, both hands looking as though they were moving to the rhythm of her feeding. Kay lay there for a while, her eyes wide open, looking straight up. Gradually she lost interest in feeding, and her mother sat her up on her knee and kissed the top of her head. Kay's eyes opened a little more and, moving her mouth into different shapes at the same time, she finally gave a very large yawn, after which she vomited a little milk back again and had to be cleaned up. The mother placed her on her left shoulder, and she started to hiccough persistently.

In this observation Kay's difficulty in waking up — i.e. coming to life — is very noticeable; it is expressed by the length of time she takes to start sucking properly, by her not searching for the nipple which her mother had to put into her mouth. Only after having sucked for a while does she wake up, find the nipple in her mouth, and actively go for it. During the first part of the feeding her eyes are closed and her hands are clenched together. The mother comments anxiously as she takes time to get started. After finding the nipple she becomes more alert, half opens her eyes, her hands and arms separate and she moves her hands rhythmically to the sucking movements of her mouth. She looks up at her mother. But she finds it a struggle to stay awake and, unable to sustain this alertness for too long, she gradually falls back into sleep as the internal pressure of hunger fades. Kay lapses slowly back into the self. She expels by vomiting, yawns, wants to be left to carry on sleeping. Her mother will not allow it and shakes her out of it. Kay hiccoughs concretely to illustrate the hiccoughs in this mother/baby relationship.

In the following observation things had not substantially improved. The mother appeared to be more and more anxious about the baby fading away and dying. This situation reached its peak when the father mentioned that they had both been quite frightened the previous evening, as the mother had gone

to Kay's cot to find that she had vomited and had inhaled some
of the vomit into her nose and seemed to be very still. The father had picked her up by the legs and banged her on the back,
and she had been all right.

The level of parental anxiety was very high indeed. At this
point the mother began to use her empathy more to predict and
anticipate Kay's needs and reactions. She noticed how some of
her interventions, such as bathing, or interrupting the feed to
change her, were upsetting Kay and reflected on how she could
improve them. This, in turn, allowed Kay to deintegrate more
freely for longer spans of time as she was able to rely on a mother
who could begin to hold her, both physically and emotionally.

> By the sixth week Kay was guzzling, sucking the knuckles of
> her right hand. Her mother was sitting in her chair and prepar-
> ing to feed her. She placed the nipple toward Kay's mouth,
> but the child hesitated and fussed before she began to suck,
> her left hand free with her fingers moving to and fro and her
> right hand resting on her chest, which could not be seen as
> the sleeve of her jumper suit was loose and not turned above
> her wrist. Eventually Kay tired of feeding, her mother propped
> her against her shoulder and successfully burped her. Kay had
> begun to use her neck muscles for she was trying to move her
> head, lifting it in spasmodic movements in order to look at
> her mother. Her mother talked about the anxieties she had
> experienced since I had last seen her. She had been feeding
> Kay as normal when she had vomited back the contents of
> her stomach. As the mother said, "It shot out all over the car-
> pet and the couch." This had happened more than once, and
> so both she and her husband had decided to contact the pedi-
> atrician at the hospital. He had not been unduly worried and
> said that he thought there was very little wrong except that
> perhaps she had been overfed. "Now I let her really cry with
> hunger," said the mother. "I had a tendency to pick her up
> and start feeding her before she was fully awake."

After this things at last began to improve. The mother did
some thinking about what was going wrong with the feeding
process, and she told the observer that since then she had been

letting Kay wake up and cry with hunger before feeding her. This meant that Kay had to demand her feed vigorously, and she could do this only by coming to life and deintegrating fully.

It was observed that since then Kay began to latch onto the breast in a lively and active way, and a good fit now occurred between the nursing pair. From then onwards an increasingly good relationship was recorded between mother and baby, and a full deintegration-reintegration sequence over feeding was observed. Here is an extract from an observation taken at eleven weeks:

> The mother picked her up and said it seemed that she was hungry, and I followed her to the bedroom. She settled herself against the pillows and prepared to feed Kay, releasing the flap of her brassiere. She offered the nipple to Kay, who took it without any fuss. Her left hand went up to her mother's breast and she kneaded it finger by finger, looking up at her mother and smiling with the milk running out of the side of her mouth. Her mother smiled in return, and Kay continued to suck, pausing at intervals to smile at her mother.

The interaction we observe here shows clearly that Kay now recognizes the breast as good, that the bad feelings about it — rejecting it, vomiting, and falling asleep while feeding — have receded because she no longer feels intruded into by it. She wants the breast, knows that it is her mother who gives it, and establishes eye contact with her, smiling at her during the whole feed while caressing the breast gently with her fingers. It seems that she cherishes it and knows that it is outside herself and that by calling and crying she can get it back, whereas by smiling and cooing to mother she can be smiled at in turn, held in her mother's arms and played with.

The bonding process in this mother and baby pair had taken quite a long time to become established due to the various factors mentioned above. In cases where bonding never does become properly established, however, serious psychic disturbances are likely to manifest themselves in the baby in the course of development.

REFERENCES

Barnett, C. (1970) Neo-natal separation: The Maternal Side of Inter-actional Deprivation. *Pediatrics* 46:197-205.

Bion, Winnifred, (1962). The psychoanalytic study of thinking. *The International Journal of Psychoanalysis* 43:306-10.

Bowlby, John (1973). *Separation, Anxiety and Anger.* New York: Basic Books.

Brazelton, B. (1983). *Infants and Mothers.* New York: Delta.

Condon and Sanders (1977). *Studies in Mother-Infant Interaction.* New York: Schaffer.

Fordham, M. (1969). *Children as Individuals.* London: Hodder & Stoughton.

Fordham, M. (1976). *The Self and Autism,* L.A.P. Vol. 3. London: H. Karnac Books.

Fordham, M. (1978). *Jungian Psychotherapy: A Study in Analytical Psychology.* Chichester: John Wiley.

Jung, C. G. (1930-31). "The Stages of Life," *Coll. Wks.* 8.

Jung, C. G. (1939). *Coll. Wks.* 9.

Jung, C. G. (1946). *Psychology of the Transference. Coll. Wks.* 16.

Jung, C. G. (1939). *The Concept of the Collective Unconscious. Coll. Wks.* 9, 1.

Lichtenberg, J. (1983). *Psychoanalysis and Infant Research.* Hillsdale NJ: The Analytic Press.

Peterson, G. (1978). Some determinants of maternal attachment. *American Journal of Psychiatry,* 135:168-173.

Piontelli, S. (1987). *International Journal of Psychoanalysis,* 68:453.

Prechtel, H. (1973) Personal communication.

Strauss, R. (1964). "The Archetype of Separation." In *International Congress of Analytical Psychology.* Basel: Skrager.

Tustin, F. (1986). *Autistic Barriers in Neurotic Patients.* London: H. Karnac Books.

CHAPTER 2

SEPARATION, SPACE AND PLAY

Whereas before birth the mother's body is the container of the foetus, after birth her arms and lap are the actual place for the physical containment of the infant; concurrently, her mind and her maternal reverie form the invisible container for the baby's psychic and emotional development. Throughout life, the dynamic processes set in motion at birth in the primal self will continue to modulate the relationship between consciousness and the unconscious. In the course of his individuating processes, the growing child moves away from mother into the wider world, both externally and intrapsychically. That is, as in reality he learns to relate to mother, father, siblings, and the world around him, internally he develops a relationship to an internal personal family as distinct from the archetypal one, always on stage in the "theatre of the mind" (Macdougall, 1986).

In her paper, "The Archetype of Separation," Ruth Strauss writes:

> In trying to understand the underlying motives which lead people into analysis I concluded that the basic conflicts of un-

21

ion and separation are indispensable for self-realisation. Self-realisation is largely concerned with ego growth which involves growing up and away from the original state of union — the predifferentiated self. Obviously, the image of mother and child lends itself best to represent this situation. It appears that this image or fantasy is so highly charged that it brings about the perpetual conflict between the wish to restoring the primary union and the need to growing away from it. (Strauss, 1962)

Dorothy Davidson, on the other hand, in her paper, "Playing and the Growth of Imagination," defines the emotional setting in which self-realization occurs in relation to the "image of mother and child" in the active development of the child from birth onwards:

The potential space between mother and baby is a sort of play-ground or stage. It is the place where archetypal opposites within the baby can be enacted. . . . The mother receives the play which is being enacted and contains it through her responses, allowing enough, but not too much space, thus preventing the playing from tipping over into nightmare-like experiences for the baby. Through acting as a container the mother holds the primitive phantasies and emotions of the baby. (Davidson-Tate, 1956)

The mental process described by Davidson is similar to what Bion called the "maternal reverie"— that is, the mother's capacity to accept and give meaning to the baby's emotional experience. The process of nonverbal communication between baby and mother has been defined (projective identification) by Klein. This process is at the root of all human nonverbal communication and is related to archetypal experiences in infancy taking place during the deintegration-reintegration of the primal self of the baby, which is a system open to exchanges, according to the Jungian theoretical model.

Tom Ogden has recently very clearly described and clarified the function of projective identification. He writes (1986):

Projective identification, as I understand it, allows the infant (more accurately, the mother-infant) to process experience in a way that differs qualitatively from anything that had been possible for the infant on his own. In projective identification, the projector induces a feeling state in another that cor-responds to a state that the projector had been unable to ex-perience for himself. The object is enlisted in playing a role in an externalized version of the projector's unconscious psy-chological state. When a "recipient" of a projective identifica-tion allows the induced state to reside within him without immediately attempting to rid himself of these feelings, the projector-recipient pair can experience that which had been projected in a manner unavailable to the projector alone.

Projective identification is not simply a process wherein the mother (as object of a projective identification) "metabolizes" experience for the infant (projector) and then returns it to him in a form that the infant can utilize. Although this is a com-mon conception of projective identification, this understand-ing falls short in that it implies that the infant's receptivity remains unchanged throughout the process. Without a change in the infant's way of experiencing his perceptions, he would not be able to modify his expectations even if his projection had been modified by the mother and made available to him.

The emphasis Ogden puts on the innate predisposition of the baby to change his way of experiencing his perception, when his projection has been modified by the mother, is, in my view, closely linked to Fordham's concepts of the primal self and the archetypes.

According to the Jungian view, as expressed by Fordham and the London post-Jungians, of whom Davidson is a representa-tive, the baby projects into the mother the part of himself he needs to make sense of, combined with the archetypal content of his experience, leaving it to the mother to make sense of it and return it to him in a digestible form. This same process oc-curs during the course of analysis and in other close emotional relationships in life. The ability of the mother analyst/receiver of the projection to make sense of it and return to the baby/analy-sand their projections enriched with meaning is crucial for the process of communication and cross-fertilization in the context of decoding nonverbal interchanges, insofar as the baby/analysand operates in the open system way that Ogden and Fordham describe.

By postulating a separate primal self in the baby, Fordham hypothesizes a matrix that could be conceptualized as the container of all the baby's potentialities—a sort of blueprint from which the potentialities will eventually unfold and emerge, following a dynamism that involves both body and psyche. At the start, the primal self is, paradoxically, totally dependent on the mother for its functioning and surviving. It follows that the primal self cannot function in a void but only within the containing frame of the mother ego/self dynamism, like a container within another container in rhythmic syntony.

Acquisition of the Sense of Space and Time

Piaget (1937) wrote that object, space, causality, and time appear to evolve in an interconnected fashion and cannot be analyzed without reference to one another.

The first sphere within which the world of objects is created by the baby is the area of the mouth and the encircling of the maternal arm. The experience of the encircling creates the boundaries of the body as the mouthing gives shape to objects before and alongside the senses of sight and hearing.

As we have already seen in the very early stage of extrauterine life, the appearings and disappearings of the mother/breast—in terms of presence and absence experienced by all the senses—who comes and goes, together with the infant's inborn predisposition (archetypally determined) for separation, are the major factors contributing to the baby's developing and eventually acquiring a sense of the dimensions of space and time. The infant, being unable to move, can look around and follow mother's movements until she disappears from his eyes; he then waits and looks, searching for her, eventually fixing his gaze on the spot where mother disappeared, expectantly anticipating her return (disturbed babies do not show such anticipation). Later on, when mobility is acquired at the toddler stage, a child can initiate geographical separation, but needs the mother to be around within reach in order to feel secure and be able to enjoy exploring the world without too much anxiety, which might become crippling. When the mother is able to remain there and tolerate the child's explorations, he will be able time after time to find his way back to her. At this stage "the conflict of union and separation" as described by R. Strauss (1962) "as indispensable for self-realization" is actually concretely enacted.

The notion of internal and external space seems to be acquired concurrently in the form of spinning invisible threads away from and back to the central point from where the mother is located. So, in the analytical relationship, the rhythm of losing and re-finding the nurturing and emotional contact parallels or offers an opportunity for this early experience to be recaptured. Thus while the baby can initially follow the mother's moves only with his eyes and hearing, later on, with the acquisition of mobility, a new tool is acquired by the toddler for the mapping out of space. Being able to find mother, time after time after time (as in the case of baby with the breast), contributes to the development of space experienced as "pauses" between the rhythmical disappearings and reappearings of mother. Internal and external spatial/temporal dimensions thus begin to shape themselves and be differentiated in the child's psyche. However, as analysts, we are particularly aware that there is yet another dimension, called by Winnicott the "in-between space," which is situated neither inside nor outside the child but *between* the child and the mother. It is in this invisible and yet extremely important space that cultural experiences, symbolic play and relationship occur (Winnicott, 1971). Among Jungian child analysts, Dorothy Davidson has been particularly interested in this intermediate area, which she has defined as "a sort of playground or stage where the archetypal opposites (psychic and bodily) within the baby can be enacted" (Davidson, 1979).

On this stage projections from the inner world on both sides can take place. It is an area for interaction and exchanges, where, all being well, unconscious fantasies are projected by the baby, made sense of by the mother, and then fed back to the baby in a digestible form, with a name attached to them. This takes place when the mother is functioning well enough, and is able to metabolize and humanize by cutting down to manageable size the powerful fantasies and emotions of the infant, avoiding at the same time filling up the stage with her own residual un-metabolized archetypal fantasies and emotions about mothers and babies.

In his paper, "The Psychological Aspects of the Mother Archetype," Jung (1938) wrote this very illuminating passage, which is parallel to some fundamental discoveries by Freud and Melanie Klein about the child's unconscious fantasies:

> I attribute to the personal mother only a limited aetiological significance. That is to say, all those influences which the literature describes as being exerted on the children do not come from the mother herself, but rather from the archetype projected upon her, which gives her a mythological background and invests her with authority and numinosity. The aetiological and traumatic effects produced by the mother must be divided into two groups: (1) those corresponding to traits of character or attitudes actually present in the mother, and (2) those referring to traits which the mother only seems to possess, the reality being composed of more or less fantastic (i.e., archetypal) projections on the part of the child. Freud himself had already seen that the real aetiology of neuroses does not lie in traumatic effects, as he at first suspected, *but in a peculiar development of infantile fantasy.* This is not to deny that such a development can be traced back to disturbing influences emanating from the mother.

This statement is fundamental in analytic work with children and adults alike.

The following case of a woman patient is a typical example of a negative mother complex in a young woman whom Jung would have defined as being in the grip of the archetype.

Since childhood as this young woman, Miss S., experienced her own mother, locked up in a masochistic relationship with her husband and children. Self-sacrificing, self-defeating, while at the same time resentful of them but unable to express any resentment and hatred openly, instead she persecuted her family by arousing in them dreadul feelings of guilt. In short, one could say that my patient was in the grip of an unconscious fantasy of a destructive primal scene, which prevented—using Jung's terminology—a *coniuctio oppositorum* in her psyche, that is to say the development of the *transcendent* function (see chapter 7).

Using Jung's model, in this case, the first point refers to the attitudes and problems actually present in her real mother. These could be found in the death of the maternal grandmother when her mother was only four years old, and again of her stepmother when she was eleven. These explain her mother's excessive clinging and anxieties about separating from her children. In reality she had suffered a great many losses, as she also had had two miscarriages immediately after Miss S. was born. As a counterphobic defense against separation, she used to send her children from a very young age to spend the whole summer with an aunt on an island far away, as if she were trying to innocculate them against the eventuality of her own death.

Miss S. had a sister three years younger and a brother six years younger than herself, whose births she had always deeply resented and by whom she felt pushed into a corner. She could not use her siblings to gang up against the parents when she experienced them as bad, and therefore she always felt intensely lonely.

Jung's second point concerns the peculiar development of her infantile unconscious fantasies: she had to make sense of a depressed mother, full of "dead mothers and babies inside her," who from the age of twelve months used to send her away for very long periods. Apparently as a baby she had never shown her distress, acting the brave little girl, so nobody could see what she was going through. She contained her pain, but it became somatized.

The psychic pain and emotional deprivation that these circumstances caused Miss S. were neither understood nor made sense of by the mother, who was satisfied by the apparent "easiness" of the baby; as a result, the baby's distress became physical illnesses; her aunt would nurse her and try to comfort her but would not call her mother for fear of upsetting her. Thus my patient remembered as nightmares her solitary confinement in an alien place. She suffered unbelievable fears and panic states, during which her mother was not there. She was dead, as far as the baby was concerned. She felt that nobody could help her and nobody really cared. Her illnesses, which continued all her life until she came to analysis, were very serious ones and often she came near death. It is interesting that since she got in touch with her psychic pain, her somatizations have stopped — as in the case of Robert, the little boy whose case follows.

Miss S.'s inner family constellation contained, as I have already said, a destructive primal scene. The father appeared in it as a very dangerous monster who could damage the mother and the babies unless he was kept out and fenced off. He appeared in her dreams as a frightening figure, looking into the house from outside the front gate — therefore excluded and removed from any possibility of interacting with the other members. This scene appears to contain some of her childhood fantasies about parental intercourse, and also a wish to punish father, whom as a baby she imagined as the one who enjoyed mother's good breast when she was sent away — a preoedipal fantasy, which, in the case of my patient, became "real" due to the actual experience of abandonment. In the session she spoke of her real father as a dictator and a disgusting, greedy old man, who like an ogre had always been insatiable. She supported her complaints with long description of scenes at the family table, where he had the right to have as much food as he liked, while she was given a small portion and had to limit her appetite. Besides, mother always hovered over him and fed him as soon as he came home from work, while all the children were made to wait. The hatred and resentment in my patient's voice when she recounted these events was still very alive. She seemed locked up in a talon law mode of thinking.

The unconscious fantasies behind these descriptions belong to an oral sadistic stage in her development (twelve months). The image of the mother barricaded inside the house with all her children clinging to her while the menacing father was looking in could be interpreted as a projection of the father of her sadistic greed. Like Cronus, he appeared to want to eat them all up, or alternatively to eat up the mother's food and leave the babies to starve.

If the father was allowed into the house/mother, he would create violent disruption and damage mother's body, filling it with dead babies (mother miscarriages). With such an impossible primal inner drama being staged in her psyche, my patient could only be aware of her wish to rid herself once and for all of both these parental figures, who in her fantasy could only damage her and each other. It is interesting to note how her unconscious had tried to solve her dilemma. Since childhood, for her, being dependent and vulnerable, was an extremely risky, painful state to be in, she tried to make herself tough, independent, and totally self-sufficient. She began by rejecting her mother, who, she felt, had rejected her by sending her away. In this way, she starved herself emotionally, but she also clung desperately to her mother when she was around and in that way felt very devouring. By rejecting the mother, Miss S. both avenged herself and preserved herself from further let-downs on her part, while deluding herself that she could do without the mother because mother was useless. She further deprived and isolated herself, almost to the point of no return. She eventually became anorexic in adolescence, a phase that lasted over seven years.

It is not surprising, given her personal history, to hear that this young woman had great difficulties in establishing the right distance between herself and her close relationships, which she

experienced either as suffocatingly close or as exasperatingly distant. Upon her return from a two-month-long separation, she
had been left by a boyfriend very abruptly and unexpectedly
after a seven-year relationship. She experienced the rejection
very traumatically and was in great despair when she initially
came to see me. She was frightened and apprehensive about
the analytic commitment, and I had some difficulties in establishing the structure of a three-times-weekly analysis, as she felt
it was too much to ask from her. She did not have the money,
and besides, how long was it going to last anyway? We debated
on this point for a whole month, and I had to be very firm, as
I felt that unless she was going to settle within a stable and well-
balanced analytic framework, no analysis could occur because
of her extreme unconscious separation anxieties, for which she
compensated with a fierce pseudo-independence and denial.

In the analysis, breaks and weekends were very hard for her,
but for the whole first year she would attribute her distressed
state exclusively to the absence of her beloved, over whom she
cried buckets of tears. In no way could she see, in spite of my
interpreting it to her, any connection with my absence and her
feeling rejected by me as by the mother of her childhood when
sent away to stay with her aunt on the island. This state of affairs
in the transference did not shift until well into the second year
of her analysis, when, before my summer holiday break, she had
the two following dreams.

> She dreamt that she was on the island of her childhood, in
> the part that usually was submerged by the tide, and she was
> a child, with other children wandering in that forbidden area
> unattended. The atmosphere was sombre, the sky dark grey
> as before a storm, when suddenly a very big tidal wave rose
> from the dark sea in her direction, and she woke up feeling
> terrified and panicky. She associated the scene with summer
> storms on her aunt's island and the fact that children were
> told to stay away from the lowlands where the tide could be
> dangerous, but she would disobey and lead other children in
> the forbidden area because there were no adults to supervise

their whereabouts.

I linked the dream with her anxiety about my imminent leaving her unsupervised and the overwhelming fear (tidal wave of emotion) that this stirred up in her inner child. I also added that the dream had brought up to the surface a wave of emotions about being left, which she had so far been able to control by cutting off and denial. Her dream was informing us how it felt being left then, as a tiny child, in relation to how she was still feeling now. At last she was able this time to accept the interpretation and show distress and feelings of being in danger.

When she was a toddler, each time that she had been sent to the island she had experienced being exposed to all sorts of emotional dangers and attacks from dangerous and endangering forces in a space that was not protected by mother's presence, and therefore she had to resort to denying that any of those dangers existed in order to survive at all. But she had felt an emotional void and was extremely lonely. She cried and expressed much pain, and the whole session was very moving.

The next day she brought another dream:

> She dreamt that she was coming toward a city, which was built around a small lake. There were skyscrapers and very tall buildings, but the city was completely deserted. She was carrying a small child in her arms. The sky was very dark, and suddenly she realized that the buildings were shaking because an earthquake was beginning. She felt very frightened.

I interpreted the earthquake as symbolizing the archetypal experience of falling apart when she felt abandoned by mother as a baby.

It was clear to me that she had at last reconnected in the transference with her early fears, in relation to the impending abandonment on the part of the mother analyst. The powerful imagery and symbols—the tidal wave, the storm, the earthquake—point to an early catastrophic psychosomatic experience of disintegration in infancy. We were able to see how those images still contained the unintegrated affect of her past, yet she could acknowledge that now she was the adult carrying the child self in her arms. Yet at the thought of the break (the loss of the analyst), the place felt empty, frightening, and deserted. The working through of these two dreams brought about an important shift in the patient's inner life, as well as in her everyday life.

A young boy, three years old at the time of his referral, in his own right presented difficulties with separation and anxieties similar to those of Miss S. He was referred because he had refused to attend a playgroup a few months previously. He had developed various phobias and tantrums at the point of separating from his mother, followed by nightmares and not wanting to let mother out of his sight at any time, day or night.

There are similarities in the personal histories of the two patients; they both suffered early separation from the mother, and both mothers were depressed, having miscarried other pregnancies. At the initial interview, Robert's mother talked about having two miscarriages before Robert's birth. He was born two months premature, was jaundiced, and had to spend a week in an incubator. She told me of the difficult time he had had there, as he developed an infection and was on the verge of dying of heart failure. Later, a second baby had also been premature, and her own father, to whom she was very attached, had died two months before the birth of the second child, causing her great distress. Following her father's death she had developed some acute pains in her back, which kept her in bed for two months and which made looking after Robert very difficult as she could not carry him in her arms. Robert was breast-fed after he was discharged from hospital, and took to the breast very well, but was prematurely weaned because of the second pregnancy. Mother appeared to feel very guilty about his birth and about her not having been a good mother, having, so to speak, damaged him and the family.

Another element that was apparent in both cases was the absence of a strong father who could deal with and contain the mother and her distress; in both cases the father was experienced as a dangerous, greedy baby or a violent monster by the patients.

The aetiological factors in this case were dual, following Jung's passage mentioned above: those present in the real mother due to her pathology, and the archetypal projections, which must, in Robert's case, have been intensified by his experience of the incubator and isolation from mother at birth.

In the first session Robert had considerable difficulty in separating from his parents. He eventually followed me into the room on his own and became interested in playing with a doll's house and the farm animals. He built a stable and set up a whole scene, as on stage, taking all the cows and putting them into the stable with their calves next to them, saying it was night and they had to be safely inside. He locked all the gates and put fences around the building, saying it was not safe to leave them open. He then found some bulls, said they were dangerous, and placed them outside the fences.

I commented that babies felt safe with their mummies only if the bull daddies were kept out. He mumbled that they were males and could be dangerous.

The boy's play, as Miss S.'s dream, depicts the young baby's wish to keep mother all to himself and to fence off the father, who is experienced as a dangerous rival.

Robert carried on with the game and said there was a storm now, and it was dark and frightening. The babies were afraid and were calling their mothers because the thunder up there in the sky was so very frightening. He sounded tense and afraid. I said he was telling me how frightened he could become at night, and that it was dark and the thunder in the sky sounded like the voice of a big, angry man or an angry, fierce bull. He agreed and carried on playing, reproducing a chaotic storm in the stables. I had, by now, begun to have some idea of his castration anxieties and his fear of a violent primal scene, with the baby calf holding on to mother to prevent the imagined violent intercourse, and, at the same time, his being afraid of the father bull's fierce, retaliatory anger (figured by the storm and the voice in the sky). (The storm and other natural catastrophes also figure in Miss S.'s dream, as we saw earlier).

The theme of separation is thus being introduced in play. (Unconsciously, separation is related to weaning and teething, as Robert began to worry about cows biting him). Biting and being bitten became from this point onwards a very important theme of his analysis. Another theme which emerged—centered around separation—was that of leaving on a journey where he would be in charge and could decide who was allowed to go and who had to be left behind. This seemed to me to indicate his attempts to be in control of his separation anxieties, because he could pretend to take the "goodies" with him and leave the "baddies" behind.

My holiday breaks were as distressing for him as for Miss S., because in both of them the "infant part" felt rejected and starving in the cold. Once, when he was very angry with me after a long break, he played with the wild jungle animals—as if he could not contain his wild and fierce hunger a minute longer. He put all the wild animals into cages, he built very complicated fences and gates to the cages, and he made sure that the lions, tigers, and crocodiles were safely locked in. Otherwise, he said, they would bite if they were let out, and he emphasized that they were starved and very fierce. It felt as if those fierce animals were inside Robert, eager to bite me and eat me up, as my absence made them feel starved. He climbed onto my body in response to this suggestion, stretching his hands to reach my breasts, which he attacked by scratching and punching.

It seems to me that the material presented by both of these patients was related to early infantile fantasies colored by experiences of premature separation from the mother. They were both looking for containment—the lost good breast—and having found it within the analytic space, they were able to enact their fears and fantasies to somatize, but to understand the somatization as a bodily attempt to communicate their psychic distress. As it happened, both have become less prone to somatize as a result of such insight.

In the case of Robert, his building of fences and cages, and taking over more and more space in the room, as well as his locking me in and out of his presence, all show how he slowly became able to manage separation. In fact, after the first Christmas break and the long separation that occurred, he came back to analysis looking more together, and his parents reported that he was now attending playschool regularly, beginning to make friends and to allow his parents much more freedom. They said that his appetite had increased, and he soon began to look stronger and chubbier, more like his younger brother, and the colds and coughs did not reappear at times of breaks. A circus with clowns and animal tamers appeared instead. His sense of reality greatly improved, and with it much clearer boundaries between the inner and outer world, which enabled him to overcome many of his phobias and to talk more freely of his fantastic inner life, which he now knew was not actually reality and could be safely imagined, both with me in the room and on his own. At this point I would like to stress that Robert's ability to express himself through symbolic play, and also verbally, was above average for his age.

Similarly, in the case of Miss S., after that very dramatic dream she showed a greater true capacity for tolerating separations and be creative about them. She found herself a new job, which made her fully financially independent from her family, and she bought her own flat. She changed some of her friends — particularly those who played sadomasochistic games with her — and she could talk with me much more freely about her feelings — both good and bad — toward me. She was beginning to acquire a sense that separations and breaks are not caused by her and her unbearable badness.

In the case of Robert, the conflict about clinging and letting go was transferred to his relationship with me, and he exhibited in his play the beginning of creating an area of his own to which I was denied access; he kept on going in and out of this area. Within the room he tried to create the "space" between us about which Dorothy Davidson (1979) writes. As his analyst I was made to share with him and sit out with him a moment of total distress and overwhelming panic. My being able to stand his agonizing pain and total states of panic in a calm but concerned way, sharing his distress without giving in to the wish of comforting him out of it, enabled us slowly to manage these very difficult moments in his analysis — as had happened in Miss S.'s case. In short, I had to stand the projection of the total bad parent, and the total bad, cruel, tormenting, ruthless mother/breast, which I understood as the patients' reliving of early infantile archetypal experience in which it had been a battle for their lives.

Like Miss S., Robert had a tendency to somatize his otherwise inexpressible instinctual overflow, using this also as a way of dealing with his rage, which his parents could tolerate in this way and for which they could comfort him. At the same time, he would manage also to get away from me, who, he felt, was making him suffer.

In the course of a relatively short analysis, both these patients were able to deintegrate and to regress to the level of the early traumas that had caused them to experience disintegration. The holding of the analyst — both interpretative and beyond in the transference — as well as her maternal "reverie" (empathetic, concordant countertransference [Fordham]), had provided them with a transformative experience of solid and safe boundaries within which a satisfactory reintegration could take place.

In "The Archetype of Separation," after stating that separation is essentially paradoxical, Ruth Strauss writes:

> In my view the experience of separation is needed so as to

gain sufficient ego strength to achieve this end. Thus separation plays an integral part in the process of ego development. However, growth of ego boundaries cannot come into being without the experience of primary union or oneness. (1962)

And she thus concludes:

The basic conflicts of union and separation are indispensable for self-realization.

REFERENCES

Davidson, D. (1979). "Playing and the growth of the imagination." *Journal of Analytical Psychology, 24,* 1.

Fordham, M. (1976). *The Self and Autism.* L.A.P., Vol 3. London: H. Karnac Books.

Fordham, M. (1978). *Jungian Psychotherapy.* Chichester: John Wiley.

Fordham, M. (1982). "Some Thoughts on De-integration" [Unpublished].

Jung, C. G. (1909). "The Significance of the Father in the Destiny of the Individual." *Coll. Wks. 4.*

Jung, C. G. (1910). "Psychic Conflicts in a Child." *Coll. Wks. 17.*

Jung, C. G. (1921). *Psychological Types. Coll. Wks. 6.*

Jung, C. G. (1926). "Analytical Psychology and Education." *Coll. Wks. 17.*

Jung, C. G. (1939). "Conscious, Unconscious and Individuation." *Coll. Wks. 9, 1.*

Jung, C. G. (1939). "*The Mother Archetype.*" *Coll. Wks. 9, 1.*

Jung, C. G. (1943). "The Gifted Child." *Coll. Wks. 17.*

MacDougall, J. (1986). *The Theatre of the Mind: Illusion and Truth on the Psychoanalytic Stage.* London: Free Association.

Ogden, T. (1986). *The Matrix of the Mind.* New York: Jason Aronson.

Piaget, J. (1937/54). *The Construction of Reality in Children.* New York: Basic Books.

Strauss, R. (1964). "The Archetype of Separation." In *International Congress of Analytical Psychology.* Basel: Skrager.

Tate-Davidson, D. (1956). "On Ego Development." *Journal of Analytical Psychology, 3,* 2.

Winnicott, (1971). *Playing and Reality.* London: Pelican Books.

CHAPTER 3

THE BEAUTIFUL PRINCESS AND THE UGLY LITTLE MONKEY

The following case deals with separation anxieties in a latency girl, whom I shall call Mary, and who was nine years old when she began her therapy. I saw her for about two years—initially once a week, after six months twice weekly, and in the final stage again once weekly. I mention these details as the negotiation of the frequency of the sessions was extremely important for the outcome of the therapy.

Mary had been referred to me because she exhibited severe school phobic symptoms and panic attacks the moment she had to leave her mother. She always stayed at home, close to her mother, and she had no friends of her own age. Her sister, Lucy, who was one year older, appeared well adapted and attended school successfully.

The mother was totally unable to control Mary's behavior, and this exasperated the father, who alternated between a so-called permissive, understanding approach and outbursts of frustration and temper directed at Mary that frightened the whole family.

(This case showed some similarity with that of Robert because in both cases the parents appeared unable to manage the om-

39

nipotence of the child, and they seemed to collude unconsciously with it).

Before coming to me, Mary had been taken to a child psychiatrist who appeared to have become angry with the family's collusion, prescribed some drugs, and dismissed them abruptly.

At first my countertransference response was negative: I did not want to become involved with such an absurd family. My negative response seemed dictated by my superego, and I suspect that this is what happened with the psychiatrist.

The parents kept repeating in Mary's presence that they could not handle her, that she would not change, that she had always been the difficult child, and that although they were bringing her to me, they did not believe that she could let go of her phobias. The mother, who did most of the talking, made a long list of Mary's phobias: fear of school, of the subway, and of the car, agoraphobia, fear of the dark, inability to sleep on her own at night and always needing her mother next to her, fear of doctors, of hospitals, of dogs — the list seemed endless and was communicated in a monotonous, mournful tone of voice, accompanied by gestures all expressing failure and renunciation. The father, who looked extremely depressed and spoke very little, expressed even more helpless feelings than his wife and nodded often to her comments. The parents were both teachers, and Mary's symptoms — fainting and throwing herself on the floor in the grip of screaming fits if forced to go to school — humiliated and shamed them.

The mother had been in therapy for a severe depression with a colleague, who suggested that they should seek help for the child in her own right and referred them to me. Prior to the first meeting, I received a telephone call from the mother, and the issue of manipulation and control became immediately apparent. None of the times I could offer was any good. It took three telephone calls from her and a very firm response from me for her to be able to accept one of the times I was offering. In the meantime, I also received a telephone call from the child's teacher, pleading with me to see Mary, as the situation in school was completely out of control, and she felt sorry that Mary, whom she considered a bright and gifted girl, should appear so distressed. The teacher said that unless things improved and the child was given treatment, the school would no longer be prepared to put up with her, and she would be expelled. This, of course, would have been bad for Mary and would have enhanced her feeling of omnipotence, as she would feel uncontainable. Her father happened to teach in the same school, and he not only felt humiliated but also feared that he might lose his job.

Mary's school phobia had, in fact, exploded six months earlier, when for practical reasons she had been transferred to the school where her father was teaching. The whole issue surfaced when Mary had to get ready to be driven to school by her father. Lucy, in turn, was accompanied by the mother, who had in the past always taken Mary to school too.

The parents described the following scene, which seemed to take place every morning. Mary would refuse to get dressed. Her father would press her to get up, as he had to leave. Eventually, he would resort to trying to dress her by force. Mary was extremely uncooperative, causing her father to lose his temper and rush out on his own in a fury, leaving the mother to deal with Mary, screaming and vomiting on the floor, while the other girl had to be accompanied to school. At this stage Lucy would protest and attack Mary for preventing her from arriving at school on time, and the two girls would end up shouting insults at each other and fighting until the mother dragged them both out. She would take Lucy to school first, and then Mary. Once they reached the school, she would have to sit in the corridor with Mary in fits of panic and screams, among general annoyance. Mary would only calm down if her mother consented to take her home again.

To return now to the first interview: Mary arrived, accompanied by both parents, and she refused to come into the room with me on her own. She dragged her mother in, clinging desper-

ately to her skirt, very much as little Robert had done at our
first meeting.

Mary was a very unattractive child — there was something in
her that reminded me of a little monkey. She was skinny, tense,
wiry, and edgy, and she moved in an uncoordinated, clumsy way.
She wore thick glasses and had a very pale, yellowish complexion. She appeared quite ugly, but an intelligent look in her big,
dark, sad eyes contrasted sharply with the rest of her appearance and intrigued me. She had a little squeaky voice and an
anxious breathing rhythm. She could not sit still in her chair.

Her ugliness having first struck me, I then realized that it was
her worry about it that I had picked up. While sitting there listen-
ing to her parents' complaints and despair about her, she grinned
and tensed up, anxious and frightened, and this made me feel
very hopeless about her ugliness/badness.

So the first comment I made, addressing myself to her, was
that I thought she must be feeling awful for making everybody
so unhappy and worried. I added that it would have been all
right if she had been a baby, but a girl of her age must surely
feel bored staying at home with mother all day, with no friends
to play with. Responding to the intelligent sparkle I noticed in
her eyes, I added that I could not believe that she would like
to be considered stupid, and that if she carried on missing school,
she would feel very stupid and ignorant compared to the other
children and to her sister, who would learn so many interesting
things.

She did not say anything, but she responded to my comments
in a nonverbal way — the omnipotent grin disappeared from her
face; she bent her head and appeared reflective. So I said that
if she could make herself come to see me, we might be able to
work something out, and I could help her to return to school
and succeed there. In fact, the parents had said how good she
had always been at school before her phobia had started. Her
immediate response was that she wished she could come, but
she could not travel to me as she would have to come by sub-

way and she was too frightened of it. She had a phobia of the subway. I said that it was too bad, but if she could not come to see me regularly for a period of time, I could not help her. The parents immediately intervened, saying that they could bring her by car.

So it was agreed, and they started coming once a week by car, which turned out to be a major issue for manipulation, both on the part of Mary and on that of her parents. I would receive a telephone call, perhaps the day before, from the mother, sounding very distressed and asking me if we could change the time because the car had to be repaired, or her husband had an urgent business call just at the time of the session, or that some relatives were arriving and had to be met, or the other child had to be taken for a medical, or that Mary was feeling car-sick and could not come. It took a great deal of firmness on my part and many manipulative attempts on theirs before they realized that the time of the session could not be changed just like that. In this way I managed to stop the family session phobic behavior, and on the whole Mary did come to her sessions, arriving late and often complaining how much she suffered on the journey. I added how awful she thought I was, subjecting her to all these sufferings.

At first she did not dare to express her anger against me for making her come, but eventually this began to surface, and we had outbursts and tantrums in the sessions similar to the ones she had at school; she would go out of the therapy room and join her parents in the waiting room, screaming that she was feeling sick and wanted to go home, throwing herself about, and kicking and screaming when I made her stay.

However, one event that happened in the first interview contributed to establishing a positive alliance with me. She protested that she was so terrified that she could not sleep at night, and that this was because of the pills the other doctor had prescribed for her. I suggested that perhaps instead of the pills her mother could prepare a drink of hot milk and honey for her, and that this would help her to sleep better. She seemed very pleased with my suggestion, until her mother reminded her that she did not like milk. This indicated to me that the mother had become intensely jealous that Mary could accept something from me. It became clear that the symbiotic relationship between them was unconsciously fostered by the mother, who would sabotage any attempt on the part of anyone else to intervene. I linked this to the father's passivity and felt that the mother and Mary were unconsciously using their symbiotic relationship to exclude and castrate him. The father appeared very devalued and excluded by mother and daughters from their intense homosexual relationship. I did not respond to the mother's sabotage but turned to Mary and said that it was up to her what she did, maybe she would like to try, and I left it at that. I was surprised when at the next session she reported that the previous night she had slept well because she had drunk milk and honey, and it was good. I understood this as a sign of a potential for a positive alliance between me and the side of her that wanted to get better and could let go of the sabotaging influence of the mother, which was colluding with her pathology.

The drink of milk represented in a concrete way the stuff the baby side of her needed from me in order to grow. I commented that my suggestion to drink milk had helped her to put to sleep the frightened baby part inside her. Perhaps I would be able to help her to get free from the tyranny of this baby part, which was afraid to leave her mother and kept her always at home in control and preventing her from getting away with anyone else — father or sister. I did mention her jealousy about the fantasied parental intercourse, even if Mary firmly denied it.

When she settled in therapy she began to play with the family set. Because I knew that she had much contact with her extended family, I included a set of grandparents and more children and adult figures. She took to the family game straight away and asked me if we could build a house out of an empty cardboard box. Then she set herself to play in a corner of the room at some distance from me and turning her back to me. For a period of at least three months her play developed around the theme of "who was in which place." It immediately became clear that some "places" were very much in demand, and the little children fought fiercely to acquire them. The two little girls, who were identified as Mary and her sister, were constantly fighting over sitting on mummy's lap, each pushing the other out of it. The fighting was fierce and merciless. The Mary-doll very often appeared to be the loser, and she would comment that her mother preferred the other child.

Any attempts by the father doll to provide maternal care were contemptuously refused by both girls. Mary-doll would rather turn to grandmother for help, but grandmother would ignore her and carry on talking to mother. The two women appeared to be locked in the same kind of symbiotic relationship as Mary and her own mother. At this point Mary would turn to the grandfather doll, who seemed to have been waiting only for this moment. The child and the grandfather would get involved in all sorts of lovely games and affectionate behavior, which excluded the rest of the group. The result was that everyone else started to try to push in between them. Thus the fighting and the changing of places would start all over again, this changing of places and the disruption of the couple being the constant themes of her play. I interpreted the jealousy and rivalry between Mary and her sister for the possession of mother's lap and her wish to split up the couple that seemed to get on well and isolate itself from the group.

At home, the fiercely jealous fights between the girls seemed to completely ignore the father's marital rights. Mary had, in fact, succeeded in getting the mother to sleep in her room, while the sister had been sent to take the mother's place in bed with the father. Lucy resented this, so in the middle of the night she would get up, and they would both end up sleeping with the mother. This made Mary feel that she could not win, and this was reenacted in her play in the dolls' house. I interpreted Mary's night terrors as a means used by the baby in her to separate mother and daddy so there would be no more babies. I also added that she must feel very guilty and scared of the power she seemed to possess.

At the same time, in an interview with the parents, whom I saw on their own whenever I felt it was necessary, I emphasized that in order for Mary to stop her tyrannical behavior they should get together and agree on a tactic for handling the child's omnipotence and her conviction that she was so powerful that nobody could contain her or make her conform.

Their healthy side did try to cooperate with me, but I had to struggle with their unconscious pathological collusion, which took a long time to shift. Still, they did keep on bringing the child and allowing me to work with her, and this was their conscious contribution to the child's therapy. What was also apparent from the play was that neither the mother nor the father had emotionally separated from their own parents, and Mary's mother would give up her maternal role to run back as a baby into her own mother's lap. The family had recently moved away from the maternal grandparents, and following this the mother had developed a severe depression. She telephoned her own mother and family constantly and went to visit them frequently, often leaving her husband and children behind.

We could say that the mother's depression had happened as a result of an uprooting and physical separation from her original family and town when inside herself she was still in an undifferentiated emotional state. In the course of her analysis she started painting and revealed considerable talent. In fact, her own father was a very well-known artist. When she began to attend painting classes, Mary, who could not be taken along, resented this private area in mother's life, but mother was able to attend nevertheless.

In one session, having put the Mary-doll on the grandfather's lap in the course of play, Mary told me how much she missed her grandfather, because he was the only person who loved her more than anybody else. "You see, my mother prefers my sister, because she is prettier than me and does not make her upset." "What about grandmother?" I asked. No, she said, grandmother only loved her mother and her sister because they were beautiful. She added, "Do you know what she said to my mummy when I was born? She said that I looked like an ugly little monkey, and I was the ugliest child she had ever seen. Mummy said that she was joking, but I think she meant it. She really does not like me." Now I understood my strong dislike for her in my early countertransference: she had projected onto me the unloving, jealous grandmother, and I had introjected the projection. I asked her whether she knew the story of the ugly duckling who grew into a beautiful swan, and she said that it was one of her favorite fairy tales. From that moment onwards there was a shift in the therapy, which now focused mainly on the two opposites: the beautiful little princess and the ugly monkey-baby-self.

We were approaching a holiday, and she had started to feel very restless as I talked about my break. She tried to make me jealous by telling me all the wonderful things that she would be doing with her mother, father, and sister, and from which I would be excluded. She also said that she might visit her grandfather, and he would give her wonderful things.

It was at this stage that she sat down, saying that she wanted to do a drawing. It is noteworthy that she had told me previously that she could not draw, and she had never used the pencils I had provided for her. She ordered me to sit behind her and not to look, and she became immersed in drawing a picture. She showed it to me when she finished and told me that it was Maia (note that my name is Mara), a very powerful princess who made everybody do what she wanted; Maia wanted to pull a little girl next to her by the hand, but the girl had let go and was waiting to see Maia's reaction. She said she had plenty of pretty clothes and jewelry. I commented that Maia looked pretty fierce to me — like someone who would not like to be disobeyed. "Yes," she said, "she gets very angry." I also suggested that the little girl looked very much like Mary herself. She agreed. So I added that Maia seemed to me to represent the baby-tyrant-princess inside her, who prevented her from going to school and had tantrums as she did not want to leave mummy. Mary nodded, so I continued, saying that now she felt that I was like Maia, as I wanted to do what I liked, just like Maia, and I did not care what Mary felt about it. I said that she felt upset and did not want to be left by me. She asked: "Why do you have to go, and where will you be?" She then added, "I know where you are going," and proceeded to draw the second picture. There I was, lying on a deck-chair, sunbathing by a hotel on the seashore. When I pointed out a little figure at the window, she said it was my cat, whom I had left behind and who was waiting for my return, feeling lonely and hungry. "Just like you," I commented, adding that she wished we could go on holiday together, and that she thought that I might be going with my children and my family; to this she added, "Your children are too big." (She had met them at the front door one day). It was my cat she was jealous of, and on it she projected the baby loved by me.

At the next session she drew a third picture, which was the story of a beautiful girl called Cynthia, who went to the seaside with her friend, Bio-Beauty. In this picture she used colors for the first time, indicating that her depression was beginning to lift. She told me that they had a wonderful time and lots of fun together. I asked: "Like you imagine we could have, if I liked you best and took you on holiday with me?" She did not comment, but she added that Cynthia and Bio-Beauty were both very beautiful. I asked whether she thought that Cynthia was special because she was beautiful, perhaps like her sister. "That one, I do not know who she thinks she is. She is always teasing me and will not let me play either with her friends or her things. She always makes me cry, I hate her." She looked upset and frustrated. At this stage the theme of the rivalry and jealousy between the sisters was coming to the fore and was being brought into the transference. Mary was expressing her feelings of envy for the older, more beautiful sister, who put her down and made her feel devalued.

In Mary's case, the feeling of being ugly worsened her narcissistic wound and made her feel helpless and rejected—the ugly baby that nobody wanted. I would not want her either. The break was approaching, and how she experienced me as the mother who had left her to go to work during her babyhood. Her feelings of being ugly mirrored her feelings of being bad inside, due to the hatred against mother and rival babies inside her whom she would have liked to destroy. All this was unacceptable to her consciousness; thus she projected the badness onto her sister, her mother, and me. When I interpreted these feelings to her, I felt we had touched upon the roots of her desperate clinging to mother. This clinging represented Mary's attempt to cling onto the "good present mother," whom she loved, to prevent the "bad absent mother," whom she hated, from taking her place.

The holidays went by without too many upheavals because there was no school, but on starting the semester and therapy the parents complained that Mary's attendance record had not improved, and that something had to be done as the school had given them an ultimatum. I told Mary that I should see her twice a week, as things had not improved with her attendance and obviously the help I was giving her was not enough. She was very angry, protested, and refused to come the second time, so I told her that we had agreed at the start that I would help her to be able to attend school and that I was going to keep my promise even if the baby-Maia part of herself was being totally uncooperative and was trying to make me fail, but I would not let down the side of her who wanted help. So in the midst of her screams and protests it was agreed that I would see her twice weekly until she managed to attend school regularly, and then we might go back to once a week, which she seemed to prefer. When she realized that I was very firm, she gave in. Fortunately I managed to convince the parents to bring her, taking advantage of their positive transference to me. She was made to come, and for several weeks she would come in angry and defiant and say, "I am here, but I want to go away. I do not like you and I will not do anything here anyway." She would then run out of the room or throw herself on the floor and kick, moan, and groan for session after session.

Eventually she ordered me to sit still, close my eyes, and not move while she started playing in a corner. This stage lasted for quite a while; she became the tyrant in the room, ordering me about as she felt I had done with her, in order to avenge herself. Eventually she had enough of this game and forgot about me. She settled down in the new routine. Now I could interpret to her that the fact that I wanted to see her more often, in spite of everything she said and did to me, must make her feel reassured that I liked her and wanted to be with her.

A new phase started then in the therapy, during which Mary was able to regress in the sessions, and lots of water games developed, centered on oral anxiety. She would often talk about her sister and how much she hated her and she wished she were an only child; she often played at drowning the bad sister who despised and belittled her and did not want to play with her. I commented that maybe her sister was as jealous of Mary as Mary was of her. I talked to her about the difficulties that both she and her sister must have had in sharing their mother when they were both tiny. I said that it was then that little Mary thought that mother preferred her sister and clung onto her for fear of being abandoned, but I suspected that her sister had felt the same about her. Mary was at first struck by this last thought and then rejected it. I added that if she really thought that her mother liked her sister better, she must also hate her mother because she left her and went to teach other children, and she liked them better too.

Following these interpretations, Mary brought a lot of material to prove how bad her sister was, as if she wanted me as an ally, totally on her side. At the same time in the session she kept using water to play and drink. She would pour herself a glass of water and would drink it eagerly, commenting that water was the best thing in the world, that it brought people back to life and could do all sort of wonders like make plants grow. "And do you know," she added one day, "that without water there would be no life on earth?" Anyway, water was her best drink. I told her that she was telling me that my water-milk-breast was making the baby part of her grow like the plants, and this would make her feel more alive and happier because my water-milk was good and was like a good mummy's breast when she was a baby.

During this period Mary's attendance at school improved. This was facilitated by her very good teacher, who made her feel welcomed and tolerated a great deal of difficult behavior from her. As things improved at school, Mary would report her successes to me and feel very proud of herself. Her parents were very pleased and were in awe of me. They thought I must have some magic powers, and for a while they kept bringing all their friends and relatives with various excuses to meet me when they accompanied Mary to her sessions, which made her sister incredibly jealous and envious. She started saying that she needed to come to me for therapy too. Fortunately this wave of enthusiasm and invasions subsided, and things went back to normal.

It seemed to me that the management and containment offered by the second session made it possible for Mary to internalize a solid container/analyst who could help her deal with her omnipotent tantrums while making her feel held and accepted by the mother analyst in spite of all that. She could begin to feel herself lovable, and this showed in a new concern about her looks and her clothes; indeed, she began to look much prettier, and she became more relaxed and more resourceful. In the transference, I was now the envied beautiful mother/sister whom she needed to beat. The competition on her part was very fierce. She would not come to the session if her mother did not give her the clothes she wanted to wear. She would comment on my clothes and ask me what I thought about hers. I interpreted what I felt was going on and stressed that she seemed to be concerned with her wish to be more attractive and beautiful than me and any other girl, so everybody would admire her, because she needed to feel good about herself inside and appreciated and admired by me, as when she was a baby she had wished her mother and father to appreciate her.

From a conversation with the parents, it then emerged that at the time of her birth the mother, who had not wanted another baby just then, had become depressed and disappointed because she would have preferred a boy. At the time she was also working full-time as a teacher, so from a very young age Mary was looked after by a variety of people and finally by a neighbor at her home, whom she hated and who frightened her. Mary remembered this woman as a sort of witch who "lived in a black house." The black house seemed to me to represent the little child's depression, fear, and sense of abandonment and lack of protection when her mother was away. She told me that she remembered having cried and cried, but nothing changed, as the mother would keep leaving her there in the morning to go to work with her children at the school. She felt that nobody cared about her misery. I thought that the origin of her school phobia could be traced back to her babyhood experience of having been left by the mother. (Note that the sister was already going to nursery school, and Mary watched her and her mother go away together every morning). At that time she began to cling for fear of losing her, but this was not understood by the mother, who felt irritated by such behavior and pushed her further away. She would then eventually feel guilty, and in order to make it up, satisfy all Mary's most impossible whims.

Since the infant within Mary could not be contained, her omnipotence was blown out of proportion. She felt like Maia, the powerful princess who ordered people about, and this frightened her. No firm and sensible management could come from the father, who was either too passive, colluding with her in irritating the wife, or too frightening, whenever in the end he lost his temper with her. I felt that the sense of reality as represented by a sound father principle was missing in this family, so I tried to help them to constellate, with some very firm and reasonable management, the positive oedipal father in the transference. In everyday life my attempts were supported by the principal and the child's teacher, who were very helpful in introducing some common sense. The situation in the family could not function because the parental couple had been split, and in their place an incestuous child/parent couple was running the household, with the result that Mary felt very guilty, bad, unlovable, and unable to stop herself, feeling that the parents were powerless over the situation. When she was first brought to therapy, her initial resistance was due to the fact that she thought that her parents were trying to dump her on me, to get rid of her, as they had done with the sitter and later on with school. The shift toward a more positive transference occurred at the second session, and developed later when the water games and the regression took place.

During the water games, she started drawing a series of containers and often asked me for a drink of water. It was summer, and she felt thirsty, but she was also anxious about the impending holidays. However, it also pointed to her beginning to create an internal container, where the water-milk could be safely kept for times of need. Summer passed fairly smoothly, and on her return Mary brought material that focused on fantasies about primal scenes — to start with, between a sausage/banana-shaped phallic object and a mouth/vagina-like spiky orifice. Her oral-sadistic fantasies, centered around the nipple/penis, were beginning to surface. They were at this time related to her having imagined me having gone away with my husband, and also her mother and father, whom she was experiencing more as a couple in their handling of her. So at this stage her murderous oral sadistic fantasies were directed against her father and his penis, both of which had become, in combination with the mother, effective in managing her omnipotent tantrums.

By now her school attendance record was quite good; she enjoyed school, and, what is more, she had started making friends. She was appreciated because she produced good work and had become able to write very good stories, which her teacher had taken to reading aloud to the class. She felt good about herself, and she also admitted that there was a boy who thought that she was pretty and nice, and who always wanted to sit next to her rather than next to another girl, whom she had considered the prettiest in the class. While we were working on this material, which was clearly pointing toward a genital development, Mary one day brought the following dream:

> In the bathroom there was a female monkey, who lay in the bathtub. She was expecting a baby; in fact, she had several babies inside her. Her inside babies were hungry, and she did not know how to stop them from screaming. There was a bunch of bananas hanging from the wall over her head, and she would pick one after the other and eat it herself in order to feed the babies. As a result, a little later the baby monkeys were born. As soon as they were born, they would run to the bananas that were left hanging and would finish them up.

She was very intrigued by the dream. I said that the mummy monkey was full of unborn hungry babies inside, and the bananas-penises that she was taking in through her mouth served to feed them. I added that it seemed to me that this was the way in which baby Mary had thought mummies and daddies got together and babies were born.

After this session a big shift occurred. The dream of the mother monkey in the bathtub seems to have occurred at a stage when Mary was trying to identify with the mother in order to solve the mystery of how babies are born. It was the turning-point in the therapy, because she could allow the babies to exist and feel that she may be able to produce them too. In fact, she began to write her stories following the working-through of this dream. It is significant that at about this time she started noticing boys and finding them attractive, and rivaling with girl students in a more positive way through her story-writing. This was her own creative gift, and because it was appreciated by the mother/analyst and the teacher, it allowed her to feel that her insides, too, were full of stories-like-babies, through which she could compete in a positive way with her sister and with her mother's paintings.

However, she became very regressed for a couple of sessions and spent most of the time lying still on the couch. When she recovered, she drew a picture of a cart pulled by a horse, with a big oak in the landscape. There is movement in this picture. The girl is driving and telling the horse to "go," the house is separated from the stable, and although there is no color, the general feeling is one of "making a move." The last two pictures that followed are much happier. Her self-image had changed: now the princess, who still had obsessional characteristics in her clothing, looks much more like a mischievous child. I think that her last picture, of a cat, where she wrote, "I am mischief," sums up the shift from an omnipotent position to a childlike, age-appropriate mischievousness.

Both the mother's depression and the premature separation constellated in Mary's unconscious negative mother-baby relationship, which developed into a magic archetypal world of witches, nasty baby princesses, and ugly monkeys. Subsequently, because the relationship with the mother-breast affected the subsequent stages of development, at the oedipal stage the father-penis was attacked and experienced as hateful and bad. Her unconscious primal scene fantasies had remained stuck at the oral sadistic level due to her massive unconscious hatred of the bad mother who actually went away (the absent mother) at about the weaning stage. The wish to kill the "bad" babies inside the mother and the "bad" father, who, she imagined, took mother away, causing her so much distress, isolated her, and filled her up with badness and guilt. Melanie Klein, in her book *Psychoanalysis of Children* (1959), writes:

Children of both sexes believe that it is the body of their mother which contains all that is desirable, especially the father's penis. The sexual theory increases the small girl's hatred of her mother on account of the frustration she has suffered from her and contributes to the sadistic phantasies of attacking and destroying the mother's insides and depriving it of its contents. Owing to the fear of retaliation, such phantasies form the basis of her deepest anxiety situation.

In his paper, "Psychic Conflict in a Child," Jung (1910-1946) describes the case of little Anna. She was four years old when her mother became pregnant, and she experienced intense conflict around the birth. Jung writes about her attempts to arrive at a satisfactory solution:

The problem of how the child gets into the mother is a difficult one to solve. As the only way of getting things into the body is through the mouth, it stands to reason that the mother ate something like a fruit, which then grew inside her. But here another difficulty presents itself: one knows what comes out of the mother, but what is the use of the father?

The fantasy that babies get inside mother through her mouth is expressed by Anna one evening, when

. . . they had oranges for supper. Anna impatiently asked for one and said, "I'll take an orange and I'll swallow it all down into my stomach, and then I shall get a baby."
    This instantly reminds us of the fairytales in which childless women finally make themselves pregnant by swallowing fruit, fish and the like. Anna was here trying to solve the problem of how children actually get into the mother. In so doing she takes up a position of inquiry which had never been formulated before so precisely. The solution follows in the form of an analogy, which is characteristic of the archaic thinking of the child.

Jung then links this infantile, "archaic" way of thinking to myth and fairytales, and he goes on:

> In German and numerous other foreign fairytales one fre-
> quently finds such childish comparisons. Fairytales seem to
> be the myths of childhood and they therefore contain among
> other things the mythology which children weave for them-
> selves concerning sexual processes.

Yet this solution to the problem did not fully satisfy Anna, because there was another puzzle: she was told that only married
women like her mother could have babies, and this could be
confirmed by the scientific observation that oranges do not become babies in her insides. So her theory was disproved, and
she had to try a new one; it was at this point that she decided
that the father had something to do with it, and, as Jung puts it:

> Hence the conviction rapidly fastened on the child that the
> father is somehow involved in the whole business, particular-
> ly in view of the fact that the problem of where children come
> from still leaves the question open of how they get into the
> mother.
>   What does the father do? This question occupied Anna to
> the exclusion of all else.

Little Anna's problem seemed to be less difficult to solve, as,
helped by both parents' support and understanding of the child's
emotional struggle, she could work through the anger and hatred for the mother who had betrayed her. In Mary's case, however, because empathic understanding from the parents was
unavailable, a situation was created as described by Klein in the
paper quoted above: "Not only do the envy and hatred [the girl]
feels toward her mother colour and intensify her sadistic phantasies against the penis, but the relation to her mother's breast
affects her subsequent attitudes towards men." It is clear from
Mary's case that the situation described by Klein had taken place,
as Mary could not trust or use her father's offers of help and
had to humiliate and devalue him all the time.

The relationship with the father could, in fact, only improve
gradually alongside her working-through of her rage and envy
of the mother. In this case the situation was doubly complicat-

ed by the mother not having worked through her problems in relation to her own mother. It was clear from Mary's early play at changing places that she had projected the good penis on grandfather, whereas her own daddy was kept bad and useless. It was only when she could feel better inside herself and had experienced the parents working together with me in her therapy that she could use her father's support and feel admired by him and creative in her own right.

REFERENCES

Jung, C. G. (1910-1946). "Psychic Conflict in a Child." *Coll. Wks. 17.*

Klein, M. (1959). "The Sexual Development of the Girl." In *Psychoanalysis of Children*. London: The Hogarth Press.

CHAPTER 4

JEALOUSY, SIBLING RIVALRY AND THEIR ROOTS IN INFANCY: THE MYTH OF CAIN AND ABEL

Cain and Abel: A Mythological Metaphor of the
Infantile Stage of Conflict

2 And she again bare his brother Abel, and Abel was a keeper of sheep, but Cain was a tiller of the ground.
3 And in process of time it came to pass, that Cain brought of the fruit of the ground an offering unto the LORD.
4 And Abel, he also brought of the firstlings of his flock and of the fat thereof. And the LORD had respect unto Abel and to his offering:
5 But unto Cain and to his offering he had not respect. And Cain was very wroth, and his countenance fell.
6 And the LORD said unto Cain, Why art thou wroth? and why is thy countenance fallen?
7 If thou doest well, shalt thou not be accepted? and if thou doest not well, sin lieth at the door. And unto thee shall be his desire, and thou shalt rule over him.
8 And Cain talked with Abel his brother: and it came to pass, when they were in the field, that Cain rose up against Abel his brother, and slew him.

61

The story of Cain and Abel is a myth insofar as it represents, in universally recognizable form, the conflicts experienced by the eldest child in relation to the birth of a baby sibling, whom — he or she feels — the parents must prefer.

In the Bible the two brothers are described as being very different: Cain, the tiller of the ground, Abel, the keeper of sheep. Cain seems to have felt that the difference in their natural endowments was the cause of the parental preference for Abel, and that, because he did not possess the gifts Abel had to offer, he would no longer be able to please his parent and obtain his love. Looked at from a psychological point of view, God's preference for Abel's offering may be interpreted as a projection of Cain's jealousy and his feelings of rejection. "And Cain was very wroth and his countenance fell." His disappointment, rage, and frustration seemed to have been extreme, as was his need to regain the undivided love and praise of the parent, his Lord. But how could he go about the latter? If he felt that he could not possibly rival the natural gifts of his brother, the best solution might have been to get rid of his brother and his talents, all in one. The thought of getting rid of Abel may have seemed to Cain the simplest solution, because at that point Abel had become for him the robber of his parent's love and the cause of his distress. Thus: "Cain rose up against his brother, and slew him." The description of the murder is very plain; it is the extreme logical consequence of a self-centered way of perceiving the universe. Cain's logic seems to have been: "If I can get rid of whatever makes me distressed, then everything will be all right again." Abel, experienced as the object causing his distress, had to be disposed of. There is no thought of the consequences, no concern for Abel. It is the father who curses Cain and persecutes him with guilt and remorse, in the fashion of a superego. If we take the myth to represent the prehistory of human consciousness, mythological figures stand for aspects of early stages of consciousness, both collective and individual. (Jung, 1939; Neumann, 1954). One could easily compare Cain's universe to the self-centered universe of a young baby, for whom his own needs are absolute, and distress and frustration are unbearable.

With this mythology in mind, let us look at the actual world of the infant and of the young child as it has been described by students of Infant Observation seminars.* The cases described here are observations of everyday life situations in so-called "normal" families, where the toddler's jealousy and rivalry feelings toward the baby sibling are clearly observable, as well as his/her distress and psychic suffering for the partial loss of the mother.

The actual drama and battles described by the observers in this chapter correspond to the inner drama that our child and adult patients bring to us in the consulting room when unresolved sibling rivalry and jealousy conflicts have to be worked through.

Anna and Liza

The first story is the one of Anna (the baby) and Liza (the toddler). Liza was 18 months old when Anna was born. Being so young, she was still in great need of her mother's lap and undivided attention. She had been breastfed for nine months and had had difficulties in letting go of the breast at the onset of the second pregnancy. She may have felt pushed out, which must have enhanced her feeling of resentment and anger at the baby sister, who had now taken over the breast. In fact the witnessing of Anna's feeding at the breast was unbearable for her and evoked her strong wishes of getting rid of the baby and attacking her. The mother, on her part, enjoyed breastfeeding and had very great difficulties in acknowledging that both her children needed her at the same time. As a result she behaved inconsistently, torn between the two: she was protective toward the baby, while being very punitive toward the toddler. At the same time, her own frustration and unconscious hostility toward the newcomer always made her keep Anna in places where she was an

---

* Examples and descriptions are all taken from observations, and I am indebted to the observers for having allowed me to present them here.

easy prey to her sister's attacks. In the following observation the
baby is six weeks old.

> She returned with Anna, and sat down on the sofa, cradling
> Anna in her arms. Anna did not react, and her eyes remained
> firmly closed. Her shoulders and arms looked quite rigid, and
> her fingers were also held straight and rigid in front of her.
> Mrs. H. spoke to her softly, touching her, and moving her
> around on her knee, but Anna remained oblivious. Liza was
> quite difficult today, and whilst Anna was sitting on her
> mother's lap, she came and pinched Anna's head. Anna react-
> ed by screwing up her face as though to cry.
> Mrs. H. placed Anna over her left shoulder, and Anna re-
> mained quiet; then she resumed sucking again.
> Occasionally, Anna sucked quite vigorously, making suck-
> ing noises that I had not heard before. Meanwhile, Liza was
> again attempting to disturb her mother and Anna by trying
> to pull Anna's head. The mother was obviously finding the
> situation difficult and tried to distract Liza's attention from
> Anna. Liza sat in Anna's chair, looking and saying "tittie" and
> making crying noises. She verbalized that she wanted the "oth-
> er tittie." Anna, meanwhile, had closed her eyes. Her sucking
> was spasmodic, but she continued to hold the nipple in her
> mouth.

After a few minutes, the mother then removed Anna from
the breast, further attempts to feed having been interrupted by
Liza's attacks to her head. Anna had become restless, unhappy,
and had cried. Mother had tried to comfort Anna, but had not
thought to feed the baby sitting in a higher position, where Liza
could not reach her. She sat down again and gave her the other
breast.

> Anna took the left breast immediately. Her eyes were closed,
> and her arm lay away from the breast. She fed quietly for a
> further 7-8 minutes. Her feeding was again interrupted on oc-
> casion by Liza, who pulled her head away from the breast a
> couple of times. Anna seemed to cope with this and took the
> nipple back easily.
> After her feed, Anna soon began to express her displeas-

ure again. The mother decided to put Anna back in her pram in the bedroom.

It is clear that Liza is not contained, but also that for Anna the feeding experience contains some very unpleasant, frightening elements. She is attacked in the midst of her enjoyment of a good feed. She seems to develop anxiety signals as soon as mother or the observer sit down with her on their knees. She seems to be anticipating an attack. At ten weeks, the following was recorded:

Mother and Liza were having lunch, and Anna started grumbling in the observer's arms.

> The mother came and took Anna. Anna was crying quite piercingly now, and her mother laid her across her knee to prepare herself for feeding Anna. She placed Anna at her left breast, and Anna took it immediately. Liza then began to cry, saying "Mummy." I went to her and helped her down from her chair. Liza was very subdued, and looked tired.

Anna carried on sucking vigorously, looking into her mother's eyes and fondling the breast gently with her open hand. Liza, at this stage, was lying miserably on the floor, aimlessly pushing a toy vacuum cleaner up and down. Mother tried to distract her, directing her attention toward the observer, but she would not have it:

> Liza said "No" and continued to lie on the floor. She then complained of a pain in her tummy. Her mother sympathized with her and told me that she, her husband and Liza had all had food poisoning on Monday. Anna had now closed her eyes.
> The mother carried on talking to the observer about various things, with Anna lying contently in her arms, looking at her and making noises as if echoing mother's talking. Liza was still on her own, trying not very successfully to distract herself with toys, while the mother was ignoring her. She then got up, and taking advantage of mother's involvement with the observer, sneakily attacked Anna, pulling her feet.
> The mother asked Anna what was the matter. She looked

at Liza and asked her if she had "done anything." Liza did not answer. Her mother placed Anna over her shoulder, and gradually she calmed down a couple of minutes before she was placed at the breast again. Liza then looked at me, and placed her hand on Anna's foot. The observer said, "Gently, Liza," and she removed her hand. Liza remained sitting there subdued and began complaining of a pain in her tummy again. Her mother asked her if she wanted to get the chocolate "bunnies" from the fridge, so Liza responded by going to find them.

It will be clear by now that Liza is suffering great distress, and her negative feelings towards the baby, instead of decreasing, have increased with the passing of time. It is as if Liza's hope that the dreadful baby would disappear as suddenly as she had appeared was beginning to abandon her, and she could not come to terms with the fact that the baby was there to stay. Her attacks by the thirteenth week had become more insistent and vicious, and the mother seemed to feel more frustrated and angry and to be unable to improve this state of affairs for either the children or herself. She became increasingly punitive and strict with Liza, which in turn exacerbated both Liza's feeling of having been unjustly rejected and her murderousness toward Anna.

Anna smiled more acutely now when spoken to and reached out her hand a couple of times toward me. Liza was meanwhile playing with a "wind-up" robot. However, she stood up and, coming over to Anna, grabbed at her, tightly "squeezing" her face against her own, then scratching the side of Anna's face. Anna whimpered and tensed as mother told Liza not to do that, and then laid Anna across her knee to prepare herself for the feed. Liza again intruded on the feed by pressing her face against Anna's head. Anna let go of the nipple and screamed furiously. Liza had bitten the side of her face. Mother scolded Liza, who turned to me, looking concerned and fingering her teeth. Anna's feed became increasingly interrupted by Liza, who refused to leave Anna alone. I tried diverting Liza's attention, but she persisted in reaching out to Anna. Mother caught her arm at intervals, and at one stage Liza, unable to get to Anna, dug her teeth into her mother's hand.

Liza eventually managed to scratch Anna's head. Anna cried furiously, letting go of the nipple. Her mother placed her over her shoulder, whilst speaking severely to Liza. Anna calmed down after a couple of minutes and resumed her feed. Liza, after continuing to reach out toward Anna, was sent to her room. Liza was very upset by this and stood for several minutes, insisting that she be allowed to come and pick up her robot. Eventually she left without it. While her mother was dealing with Liza, Anna had lost the nipple and was struggling to find it. Anna continued her feed; her mother remarked that she wondered what psychological effect it would have on Anna.

After this last observation the situation worsened. Liza, not being able to deal with her negative feelings by herself, nor succeeding in being helped by her mother, who could not make sense of them for her, started increasingly to somatize; she became very ill and developed a bad infection, with very high fever. The illness made her very regressed and in actual need of primary care, as if she were a baby.

In time, the illness helped Liza to recover, feeling that her mother still loved and cared for the baby inside her. However, the situation remained extremely difficult for Liza, and she developed neurotic trends that were very apparent by the end of the two years' observation. One might say that Liza managed to block her murderous impulse against her baby sister, and thus her dangerous acting-out ended, but she turned her murderousness against herself. In sparing the sister from her attacks, she became the victim of her own destructive wishes. It was as if she were making a statement which her mother never decoded: it was all too much for her, and she wished to do away with herself if that other baby were not removed and her loving mother restored exclusively to her needy baby self. With her attacks against herself she could punish both her mother, by making her feel guilty of not being a good mother for her, and herself for the destructive murderous wishes against her rival.

Albert and Dick

This next case presents us with an opposite situation. It raises the questions: what would have happened in the Bible if God had preferred Cain's offerings to Abel's? How would Abel have reacted? I feel this second observation might give us clues to answer this hypothetical question.

The baby, Albert, and his elder brother, Dick, who was three years old at the time the observation began, had a mother who did not like babies and found it very difficult to deal with her second-born. This was also because, as it appeared later on, she did not welcome a second boy, or a second child. From the very start the observer became aware of the mother's unconscious hostility toward the baby, which manifested itself in various ways. She did not appear to be in tune with the baby's signals; she was terrified of breastfeeding him, although consciously she was trying hard to give him the breast. She developed cracked nipples, which made the feeding situation very difficult for her, and very unsafe and unreliable for Albert, who was always held at distance from her body, in what appeared to be an uncomfortable position. He had to adapt to a struggle with a breast that seemed to want to be left alone, while he wanted and needed badly to attack it in order to feed. During the feeding, mother constantly watched television. Albert's struggle was distressing to watch: he vomited and stuffed himself in a very anxious manner, which induced stomach aches and made him very uncomfortable. The feeding situation was fraught with negative feelings for this nursing couple.

He was weaned to the bottle at around three months, the reason given being that mother's milk was not enough for such a big, hungry baby. Mother kept watching television while feeding him, and as soon as he was able to hold the bottle he was left to get on with it by himself. The elder boy, Dick, could sense all this and was not unduly jealous of the baby in such a situation. The mother was also clearly indicating that her attention was on Dick most of the time, talking and interacting with him while handling Albert. Dick, in fact, appeared to feel guilty of this and behaved protectively toward the baby, whom he never attacked. If Albert was crying and his mother delayed her response, Dick made her more aware of Albert's demands.

Mother did not talk, smile, or play with Albert, except during the bath and diapering situation, which became very erotic and exciting for Albert, who was otherwise unable to get hold of his mother. For the rest of the time he was not carried about in her arms but left to sleep in his cot or sitting in his baby chair, distant from mother, whom he could watch playing with Dick. Dick included Albert in the interaction, while mother tended to find him frustrating and excluded him.

The father was a very warm and kind man, who seemed to perform a cuddly and affectionate maternal role, not only for Albert, whom he liked to hold and fondle, but for the whole family. Thus the three of them waited with anticipation for father's return and competed for his love and cuddles.

Albert developed into a very strong, muscular baby, who crawled and moved about early, with the goal to reach mother and the wish to grow out of the helpless baby stage as quickly as possible. He started following his mother and brother around, but this was too much for mother, who erected a wooden barrier, stopping him getting to her and confining him in a small area, as she had to do housework most of the time. During quiet moments, when she sat on the sofa and relaxed, Albert was allowed to go to her, and she would pick him up while talking to the observer; he stayed very still on her lap. As soon as he expressed any affection or wish to be cuddled, she seemed to feel it was all too much for her, and usually she put him down on the floor and distracted him by giving him some active toys to play with. As a result, he usually became frustrated, and she would tease and mock him for being just a small good-for-nothing baby, while at the same time praising his brother's abilities.

Albert began to attack his brother's toys, and, as he grew more daring, he also attacked Dick, provoking him; violent fights be-

gan to take place. Mother, called in by the crying, would intervene and punish Dick, whom she always considered responsible for having started them. Ignoring his protests, she always
punished him. This pattern of Albert provoking Dick by invad-
ing his space, grabbing his toys and breaking them when angry,
as a revenge, induced the latter to hit and hurt him, which in
turn caused mother to intervene and hit Dick, telling him off.
Using mother in this way, Albert managed to avenge himself
indirectly against the brother he could not beat; he could also
be reassured in a twisted way that his mother was protecting
him, often pushing on his behalf the hated rival out of the way,
sending him to his bedroom as punishment.

Growing up, Albert showed increasingly aggressive and violent physical behavior in relation to Dick and to objects in his
environment. While his physical muscular behavior developed,
his speech lagged far behind, as well as his ability to sustain frustrating situations, which stopped him from playing constructively.
His main concern was in stopping Dick from having anything
to himself.

The observer witnessed this struggle for taking possession of
mother, which for Albert meant having to push his brother constantly "out" of this world (mother) in order to take over; but
even when he succeeded in doing so he hardly enjoyed any satisfaction. Mother remained elusive.

Towards the end of the observation, almost two years later,
the following was taking place:

Mother opened the door; Dick and Albert stood behind her.
Albert, who was wearing a grey tracksuit, took the observer by
the hand and led him into the living room, where the television
was on, as usual. He picked up a book and, as usual, gave it to
the observer.

> It was one of Dick's books—"The Master of the Universe."
> Mother grinned. "Here we go," she commented, meaning to
> express her boredom. Albert opened the book that I was hold-

ing for him and dropped it onto the floor; he went close to the television and said "Telly," then took me by the hand and led me to the children's bedroom, where I noticed the new bunk beds. There were some large balloons lying about, and Dick was playing with his Master of the Universe doll. Both boys climbed on the lower bunk—Albert's one—then Dick took the ladder to climb on the top one, which was his. Albert followed him, trying to stand on the same step he was on. There was some pushing and fighting between the two of them. Then Dick got on the top bunk, and Albert followed. While Dick began to play with some toys he found there, giving some to Albert, the latter, in a very provocative manner, started throwing all the toys down onto the floor and then, laughing, waited; he threw some more and then, expecting Dick's angry attack, rolled over. Dick knelt over and hit him— Albert squealed and giggled. Dick hit him harder. Albert, this time, grimaced, and started crying, and looked at the observer as if to ask for his intervention. As the latter did not move, Dick hit him again, and this time Albert laughed in a very provoking way. At this point Dick, having noticed that Albert had wet himself, called mother, who carried him away to change him. The interaction of the diaper change was quick, and mother made some sarcastic comments on Albert's wetting himself; he kicked her breast, giggling excitedly.

Mother then put him down, and he returned to the bedroom, under the bunk on which Dick was standing, indicating that he wanted to get on, but, as the observer did not pick him up,

Albert led me into the living room. Mother was on the telephone, speaking to her mother. Albert walked to the toy cupboard, then back to me, taking my hand and leading me back to the bedroom. He climbed onto the bed. Dick asked me to put him onto the top bunk. I did so. He pulled tape off the corner of the plastic sheet and threw the end over the side, "fishing." Albert climbed onto the shelf of the lower bunk, with his back to me, looking over his shoulder, indicating to be put onto the top bunk.

At this stage, the mother returned to the room, and her mood had changed. As she began to speak about the end of the ob-

servation, she noticed all the toys on the floor and asked Dick
to pick them up; as he was not fast enough in doing so, she became increasingly angry and hit him, while Albert, who was the
one who had thrown them all on the floor, was sitting quietly
playing with his blanket on the floor, seemingly ignoring the
scene.

> Mother told Dick to get out and take Albert with him while
> she cleared up. Dick walked out of the doorway. Albert fol-
> lowed, dragging the blankets.

This very sad image of Albert dragging his blankets seems to
me to show how Albert, although managing to get his brother
hit by mother and spoiling things between mother and Dick,
could not manage to have the good relationship with her that
he so much seemed to want and need. He failed to become a
"good loved and wanted" baby for her.

An Adult Patient

A young mother in her thirties was referred to me for depression and marital difficulties. She appeared to me to be very split
off from her emotions and childhood memories at the start of
her treatment, and looked very doubtful as to whether she wanted therapy at all. She spoke about her husband, with whom she
had a difficult relationship, in a way that reminded me of a rival
sibling. I pointed this out, but for a long time it did not make
any sense to her. Gradually, however, she started talking about
her childhood and about the time when she was eleven, when
her parents were divorced. She was called by a paternal uncle,
the head of her extended family, and told that from now on she
had to become the head of the family, as she was the eldest child;
she was to help mother in taking care of her three younger
brothers and set them a good example. (It is interesting to note
that the patient now had three children herself). She felt that
she had to show everyone how good she was, and, from that time
onwards, she had behaved as the "good girl, sister, and daugh-

ter" she felt she was expected to be. In this behavior, which carried on in her own marriage later on, there was no room for her rebellion or for any negative feelings. She felt that she had to be a self-sacrificing wife and mother, but at the same time she also felt that she could not cope with this role any longer.

As the treatment carried on, I felt that she wanted to also impress me with her heroic behavior. When I mentioned this, she justified it with reasons based in reality, such as making the most of her sessions and so on. She seemed totally uninterested in my other patients, but very concerned about not causing me any trouble or aggravation.

She eventually began to talk about her mother during the time she was expecting her youngest brother; how unwell her mother had been, and how much she had helped, bringing her mother medicines in bed, and also big glasses of pressed blood (a regional remedy for anemia, made of blood pressed from beef steak) to drink, which, she added, revolted her. I interpreted that she seemed to have felt that the baby inside her mother was like vampires drinking her blood, and she had tried to give some of her own life's blood — or energy — in order to help her mother survive, but it was at great cost to herself. I also mentioned that she might have felt angry with such greedy babies who were making her mother so weak and were eating her up from inside.

The following session she brought a dream:

> She was combing her eldest daughter's hair, and she discovered some lice. She became very excited and started crushing the lice between her fingers with real murderous pleasure. She wanted to kill them all.

She told me about the real episode in her eleven-year-old daughter's life when she had had to be disinfested, as she had caught lice at school. She was puzzled by her own pleasure in crushing the lice in the dream. I said that it seemed to me that she was crushing the greedy-baby-sibling's thoughts out of her child-self-head, as she had wished to do but could not even think about

when she had been a child. She seemed to agree. A great deal
of material that now began to emerge was very relevant to her
problems in the present, and focused mainly on jealousy, rivalry, and hatred of her rivals. She was in great rivalry with me,
even trying to make me feel jealous of her husband analyst, who
was Freudian and who seemed to be stricter in that—as she put
it—he "would not let her get away with anything."

The husband had taken the place in her unconscious of the
hated siblings which she, like Cain, had to get rid of in order
to win parental love. In this case, the unconscious and unresolved
sibling rivalry between the patient and her husband resulted in
a failed marriage—a metaphorical reenactment of the myth of
Cain and Abel.

REFERENCES

Jung, C. G. (1939). *The Archetypes and the Collective Unconscious. Coll. Wrks.* 9, 1.

Neumann, E. (1956). *The Origins and History of Consciousness.* Princeton: Princeton University Press.

CHAPTER 5

THE SHAME OF BEING "A BABY"

Webster's Dictionary defines shame as "a painful emotion excited by a consciousness of guilt, shortcoming, or impropriety." The emotion of shame has its beginnings during childhood, and it seems to arise out of the young child's recurrent experiences of his shortcomings, inadequacy, and dependency, which accompany his attempts to find out about himself, his mother, her body and his own, and the world around him.

It is necessary to distinguish between feelings of shame and feelings of guilt; the two often occur together, as they have certain elements in common. Due to such shared features, the shifts between these two categories are difficult to detect: "Shame involves attention directed to a specific self-image, i.e. the person recoils in shame over some defect represented in the image. The guilty person attends to his or her action, not to a self-image. By action is meant any production for which the person holds himself or herself responsible, whether a real action or a fantasied unconscious one" (Miller, 1986).

In the experiences connected with growing up, frustration is unavoidable, because even in the best of situations there is a gap between the child's subjective feelings of his needs and the mother's more-or-less empathic understanding and capacity to satisfy them. In infancy this situation is most acute, and it leads to the growing infant slowly experiencing the negative side of dependency, that is, feelings of impotence, helplessness, rage, and despair — factors that differ from one baby to another according to their individual resources. Frustration is made more tolerable by omnipotent fantasies of self-fulfillment or by splitting, the good object with its "good" attributes being retained and the "bad," frustrating ones being pushed away as far as possible from the self, or vice versa — in the attempt, as Tom Ogden puts it, "to separate the endangered from the endangering . . ." (Ogden, 1986).

The deep structures associated with life and death instincts lead the infant to organize experience in terms of anticipated dangers — reflecting the operation of the death instinct (see Grotstein, 1985) — and anticipated object attachments — reflecting the operation of the life instinct. Bion (1962a) described the pathological degeneration of object-related fantasies of danger into a sense of "nameless dread," which occurs when the mother is unwilling or unable to process the infant's projective identifications.

Inner and outer space are not yet defined for the baby, but a preconception that distance protects from danger seems to be innate and inherent in the psychic defensive mode of splitting, just as it is in the physical mode of flight.

These are the earliest attempts at managing frustration and making it bearable. However, as growing up occurs and with it the child's developing sense of reality — that is, in a psychologically healthy situation — omnipotent fantasies recede, and the baby has to face and come to terms with the fact that he and his mother are two separate people and that she is the more powerful of the two. A situation of trust has to be established, while his feeling of being separate increases in him the awareness of his needs, as does his anxiety whenever he feels small, impotent, and vulnerable and cannot really make things happen the way he wishes. In the best of cases, with parental care, tolerance, and support, the little child can accept this painful state of affairs. The omnipotence and the magic powers are projected onto the parents, who by containing them eventually lead the young child to manage in a realistic way his feelings of inadequacy and guilt. Because a child is not aware that he will outgrow each of the developmental stages, his shortcomings related to each of them tend to make him feel guilty and devalued, ashamed of his smallness, envious of his bigger and more powerful parents, and wishing to grow up quickly.

Usually, between the end of the first year and the end of the third, the toddler, having already mastered great skills, is struggling to manage his impotence and omnipotence alternately. His sensitivity to feelings of shame and guilt at this stage is at its highest. For a toddler to integrate hopelessness and helplessness proper to a realistic sense of self-esteem, a great deal of containment and support is needed from his parents. A supportive and tolerant attitude on their part toward his failures will help to mitigate these "painful emotions," since, at the same time, the child's ego has to cope with attacks by the superego, which, in early life, is punitive and based on talon law and tends to shame the ego ruthlessly.

When the parents act out their own omnipotent fantasies, they tend to be experienced by the child as being allied to the superego against himself. In order not to feel too ashamed about himself, he will need to disown his weaker side and to split it off, using projective mechanisms to push it outside himself. In such instances the shadow thrives at the expense of the ego, and development becomes one-sided; independence, pseudocompetence, and toughness are prematurely assumed by the child aiming at successful adaptation, at severe cost to his psychic health.

Lilli

The case history of a small girl called Lilli, who has been observed from birth by a member of the Infant Observation Seminar in London, shows the sorts of frustrations a baby can go
through and the fluctuation of omnipotence and impotence in
everyday life. Lilli was a lively child, very bright, intelligent, and
generally healthy, the second child born to loving and dedicat-
ed parents. They were both social workers and very intellectual. A sister five years older was already attending school. The
house was full of books, the parents being quiet people who tended to sit and read most of the time when they were at home
by themselves. They also read to the children. The mother did
not play with Lilli, but she read story-books to her. Reading and
educational activities were considered by the parents as more
valuable than sheer, purposeless play. It was clear to the observer that Lilli was frustrated at being the baby and was desperately trying to be a "grown-up girl." At the age of fourteen months,
just when Lilli was being weaned, her mother reported the following to the observer.

> The Mother said that Lilli has been through a bad patch — it
> lasted about a fortnight and started, she thought, with a bad
> fall in the playground, when she was hit by the swing on which
> her sister Ella had been swinging. The two children had been
> out with the au-pair girl. Lilli had had a nasty bruise on her
> forehead and a cut on her chin. She had not been happy while
> they were on holiday the previous weekend, and she became
> quite hysterical one night, when she seemed desperately to
> want the breast, but the mother said that now she had only
> sufficient milk for one feed a day. There were many things
> that seemed to displease her. The mother said that she seemed
> terribly eager to get exactly what she wanted and was desper-
> ately upset if she did not get it right — quite small things, like
> wanting tea rather than juice.
>   On the same day Lilli walked off into the house and down
> the corridor, in a very purposeful way, showing off, I thought,
> what a good walker she is. She stopped at the two steps down

into the kitchen and had to sit down in order to clamber down.
She stood up again and walked up and down the kitchen, hiding behind the dresser and then coming back. I sat down on
a chair by the table, and Lilli stood up on the chair opposite.

A couple of weeks later, during the course of another observation, Lilli picked up a book from the table and brought it to
her mother. She sat on her lap and turned over the pages while
mother pointed out different things, such as animals or babies,
in the pictures. It was quite a grown-up book about the Christmas story.

At one point Lilli got up and clearly wanted me to see the
book. However, the book had been closed, and Lilli waited until mother found the page and then brought it over to me.
She took the book back. Then she went over to the bookcase.
Mother picked her up, and she pointed to a box that she wanted, which belonged to Ella, her sister, and consisted of small
pieces of felt that could be made up into animals. Mother said
it was too complicated for Lilli, but they played with it for
a while. Then Lilli found her toy post office van. She opened
the door and took out the shapes, then put them back again,
and, with mother's help, got one or two back through the hole
(the shapes have to be fitted to the holes). She managed to
do one herself and was thrilled and clapped her hands. We
both said how clever she was; she did it again, and again we
praised her and she clapped her hands.

It was clear that she felt her sister's books were best, and it
was only after she had been allowed to play with them that she
turned to her other toy, which obviously gave her more satisfaction. She was allowed to feel proud of herself, and satisfied
with her achievement, and not laughed at when she could not
manage to do something.

The following observations took place at twenty-two months.

Mother began to cook. Lilli pointed to the wall, where there
were a lot of pictures and drawings done by Ella. Mother indicated one that Lilli had done when she was 20 months old—

it looked quite impressive. She thought her children were ar-
tistically gifted. A few minutes later Lilli stood up in her chair
and began to make some unspecified noises. Mother asked
if she wanted to make a poo. She nodded her head, and mother asked her if she would like her to get her potty. Again Lilli
nodded her head, got down from her chair, and came over
to me. When mother returned, she took off Lilli's pants and
diapers. Lilli then went over and sat on her potty, looking very
solemn until she had performed, when she stood up with a
little smile. Mother proceeded to clean her, and Lilli assisted
in the proceedings. Mother removed the potty, and Lilli began running around, getting quite excited as she marched up
and down in a seminude state, or ran from one end of the
kitchen to the other. It was quite clear that her admired painting and her successful potty training were linked in Lilli's
mind. She felt proud of both.

As we can see, a loving and caring attitude on the part of her
mother had supported Lilli in her difficult struggle to grow up.
The mother valued her efforts, did not on the whole put her
down because of her failures, and tended to praise her successes and encourage her in all sorts of ways, as it was clear that
Lilli easily blamed herself and her mother when things, as her
mother put it, "are not exactly as she expects them to be."

A nonshaming parental attitude enables the child to build inside her a benevolent and helpful superego authority, to own
her inadequacies and her "bad" side and integrate them into her
ego structure, thus preventing excessive splitting. It contributed to Lilly's achievement of a realistic sense of self-esteem and
enabled her to take pride in herself; successes such as these help
ego growth and integration.

Shame and Its Relation to the Social Context

Shame is always linked to an individual experience that takes
place within a social context, be it in relation to the mother,
the father, siblings, childhood school friends, or, as an adult, to
society as a whole.

For shame to be experienced, it seems necessary for a baby to have developed an ego sufficient to be able to acknowledge himself and his mother and other people in the environment as being separate and endowed with certain good or bad attributes. This occurs gradually but is usually established toward the end of the first year of life, reaching its peak in the various phases of toilet training and during the Oedipal stage. In the latter, jealousy and rivalry of the parent of the same sex are at their highest and are accompanied by feelings of shame at one's own inadequacy. In the course of comparing how much more the rival parents and the desired one can offer each other, the child suffers great anguish, feels rejected, and envies the couple, but also feels guilty and ashamed about it.

Not much has been written by Jungians specifically on the subject of shame. Jung himself linked feelings of shame caused by the experience of one's own inadequacy and the shadow archetype. More recently, Peer Hultberg has written about feelings of shame he encountered in his adult patients and of the difference between cultures of shame and cultures of guilt (Hultberg, 1988).

Several papers on shame have been written by psychoanalysts, following Freud's view that shame functions principally as a reaction formation against exhibitionistic impulses. In his view, prohibition against exhibitionism drives the ego to create a shame feeling that obliterates awareness of the forbidden wishes. In her recent book, *The Experience of Shame*, Susan Miller (1986), reviewing the Freudian literature, states that

> Kohut appears to understand shame as a feeling state that functions (in combination with states of self-consciousness and hypochrondriacal worry) to ground a person who is overstimulated by feelings of omnipotence.

Miller continues:

> Piers and Singer believe that experienced shame can occur

in response to any discrepancy between one's ideals and one's actual behaviour. Such a disparity between ego ideal and perceived actual self can occur in any area of functioning, be it sexual performance or moral integrity.

Grinker (1985), according to Miller,

> sees shame as the response to failure to master a development task at the normally expected time. He does not reduce shame over relatively late developmental failure to a mere reverberation of some early failure, e.g. of genital self-esteem. . .[He] hypothesizes inherent standards of functioning in the maturing person that can lead to shame feelings as early as the first year of life, for example, in response to motor difficulty. . . .[He is] sensitive to the growth-defeating potential of shame feelings when such feelings push a person to strive for unattainable ends. Grinker attributes the suicide of one of his patients to intense shame over inescapable developmental failure. The dilemma of some inalterably impaired individuals is that one cannot change but one cannot tolerate being what one is. Because the healthy child retains the promise of the future development, he or she can generally tolerate current self-dissatisfaction.

Grinker's views are interesting and correspond to my own theory that there is an emotion that sets in very early in childhood. In the course of infant observation, we have noticed individual children dealing with these painful emotions by adopting defence mechanisms that help to mitigate the anguish, the frustration, and the blow to their narcissism. Two tendencies are, however, commonly experienced: regression into the babe-in-arms stage (a turn backwards) in order to avoid the conflict, or a premature independence, a jump ahead of the conflict in the hope of overcoming it. Both are unsatisfactory as they tend to lead to loss of ego development and to pathological splitting rather than to integration, working through and assimilation of the dark aspect.

Thus the assimilation of the shadow is a necessary task for all beings. About this aspect Jung (1951) writes:

Although, with insight and good will, the shadow can to some
extent be assimilated into the conscious personality, experience shows that there are certain features which offer the most
obstinate resistance to moral control and prove almost impossible to influence.

Within the family the bucket full of dirty diapers (shadow)
is passed on from the older siblings to the younger ones, often
with merciless cruelty, as the latter represent the "messy stage,"
over which the older ones have just managed to triumph.

This also occurs when, because of their own unresolved
conflicts, parents, and adults in general, project the shadow of
their inadequacy, shame, or guilt onto the child and so contrib-
ute to the latter's feeling that he is inadequate because he is
small. As this is a fact the child has to live with, he suffers severe blows to his narcissism, feels ashamed of his smallness, and,
by overidentifying with grown-ups, he tries to compensate for
his inadequacies. Indeed, there is much praise for "good children" who never cry, are well-behaved, and act like little adults
both at home and in social life. Smallness is equated with inadequacy and mess, and bigness with competence.

As the child moves out of the family into the wider world,
he will be shamed at school by teachers and older students, who
elicit shame as an effective emotion in order to control his behavior. Although this varies from culture to culture, it is widely
employed as a means of controlling behavior.

The shaming and denigration of weakness and overpraising
of strength and power are, however, even more extreme in collective structures such as social institutions (political, religious,
military, and professional organizations) and tend to be experienced by the child via the collective unconscious of the
parents.

In the same way as a young baby would "split his object" in
order to do away with its frustrating element, which has become
equated with "badness," a group can become intolerant and frustrated with its shameful and messy side, projecting it onto a weak-

er group nearby. It may then attack the group, carrying its own shadow projections with the aim of doing away with its shadow outside "there." The majority of collective conflicts, leading in extreme cases to wars, are caused by shadow projections. In such cases the shadow archetype is activated but disowned because of the sense of shame and guilt that it engenders.

It would now be useful to explore, with the support of clinical material, the links existing between the collective and personal shadow, the emotion of shame, and its reflection on the life of an individual.

The Wise Old Man and the Messy Baby: A Pair of Opposites, Big and Small

Our starting point, with respect to the case of a five-year-old boy called Ricky, is Jung's (1957) statement, "Nothing is more disillusioning than the discovery of one's own inadequacy."

Ricky was referred to me for therapy at the clinic, where I initially saw him twice weekly. The symptoms reported by the parents were lying, soiling, heavy swearing, destructive attacks on toys and furniture in the home, desperate clinging to his father, and difficulty in concentrating at school. He also exhibited speech problems, and at times his words were incomprehensible. His parents had divorced when he was three. His mother had left the home, leaving him and his two older brothers (five and nine at the time) with the father, who was a very caring man but unable to look after the children. A year later the father had married a young divorcee with a seven-year-old son.

Ricky's symptoms worsened from the time the stepmother appeared on the scene. Recently anxiety about him, both at home and at school, had escalated to such a degree that the family and the child psychiatrist came to feel that if all else failed, hospitalization might be necessary.

When I met Ricky for the first interview, he appeared lively, warm, and responsive, but he looked persecuted, tense, muddled, and confused. He entered my room accompanied by his stepmother and the social worker. He was a very tiny fellow, with a large head set on a disproportionately thin and small body. His face was pale and wrinkled, like that of an old man. This older-man appearance was reinforced by his holding himself upright and pacing stiffly up and down the room, carrying a book under his little arm, like a "big man" with his daily newspaper. Despite this "big act" he looked very frightened, tense, and uneasy; he crouched on the floor by his stepmother in search of protection, well away from me and turning his back to me. At one point, while his stepmother commented on an improvement in school, he turned around and looked into my eyes, giving me a real, good look. He seemed reassured, accepted the paper and pencil I was offering him, and moved closer to me to display his writing abilities. Then, as soon as his stepmother moved on to talk about problems with him at home, he began to draw a house. At first it was a small house, where he, the father and the two brothers lived. He portrayed his middle brother just like himself, with a very large head and big ears, and scornfully called him "big-headed and big-eared." There was no mother in the house. The two brothers were at the windows, while he drew himself and his father holding hands going through the front door. The house looked as if crammed with bodies, so I commented that it looked a bit small for all those people. He then drew a bigger house next to it where the people had more space, but again with no female figure in it. His stepmother, who had been watching him drawing, commented on the absence of the mother and, taking it as an attack on herself, added, "He is exclusively attached to his daddy and pushes me away." I suggested that therapy would be able to help with that problem and went on to make arrangements for treatment. By now Ricky had settled in the room and was exploring the toys. He had moved away from me and was playing with the doll's house, arranging the furniture in the various rooms, very concentrated and quiet.

At the end of the session Ricky's omnipotence manifested itself. He collected the drawings he had made and told me he was going to take them home to show his dad. I suggested he leave them here, but he baffled me by marching out of the room with the drawings under his arm, looking like an executive with his work projects. I realised he was provoking me to a battle. As, at that stage, I could not interpret his behavior, I decided to let him have his way. He had gone outside and I had reentered my room when, suddenly, he ran back into the room, kissed me good-bye, and rushed out of the door again.

Note that his approach to me had occurred after his step-mother had spoken of his writing. When she mentioned his problems (shortcomings and inadequacies), he drew the house excluding her, thus displaying his wish that the father would get rid of her. At the end of the session he did the same with me. He was not taking any notice of what I said; he was only concerned with his father and wanting to please him.

At the following session, Ricky sounded very confused about me, which puzzled him a great deal and made him very anxious. It seemed to be a projection of his own anxious and confused feelings about his own identity, and everybody else's. I commented about it to him, and a flood of muddled-up, confused questions to himself burst out of his mouth, leaving no time for any answers on my part. How many mothers did he have? He told himself he had an "old mum" and a "new mum." He seemed to ask me which was his real mum. How many brothers did he have? This confused him too. Then he said that his old mum had a brother living with her, was he his new dad? Who were all these people? Who was he? Who was I? All these questions seemed to pile up in Ricky's mind, and he could not get any answers.

He was hopelessly mixed-up and insecure. I began to feel that confusion and the mental mess of muddling everyone and everything up was his defensive response maneuver against helplessness and unbearable anxieties of not knowing of being a dependent baby. It was at this stage that his language also became muddled and incomprehensible. However, he would swiftly come out of this confusion, shifting to a precarious identification with "the big-man-father," as when he looked like a man going to work, or when he used reading and writing as a way of proving his abilities to me and to himself in an attempt to deny and fend off the chaotic feelings of the baby inside himself. Thus I found myself during the whole of his treatment having to work with the pair of opposites — big and small — where "big" meant a state of idealized order, power, knowledge, and invulnerability, whereas "small" was equated with messiness, helplessness, and vulnerability.

This is, of course, quite a usual characteristic of the way small children think, due both to their experience of reality and to the interplay of archetypal projection, their own and that of the parents, which is quickly constellated in the transference. However, in Ricky's case the polarization between big and small had reached such a high degree of automatism that it obscured all other pairs of opposites and blocked the natural developmental processes of deintegration-reintegration. He could not tolerate and allow a full deintegration to take place for fear of remaining a "helpless, messy baby" forever — hence his defensive shifts from baby to old man, both in the treatment and in real life. In fact, his father and stepmother, too, had great fears of showing their vulnerability and helplessness and projected an image of self-denial, strength, and ability in order to cope even with the impossible. Thus they identified with the wise old man/woman, while the mother who had left and Ricky had to carry their projections of incompetence, weakness, and uselessness. At the same time, Ricky's behavior shamed them, as it was intolerable for them and prompted them to do everything possible to help.

In the early phases of the treatment I felt that there was a great deal of Ricky's "big-boy" act that had to be allowed by me in the transference, and I restrained my interpretations about his other side — the messy baby — in order not to shame him and add to his persecutory guilt. I made occasional comments about

his wish to show me how good and competent he was at his
schoolwork, in order not to make him feel attacked and persecuted by interpretations aiming at drawing his baby side to the fore.
I felt I should wait for his "inner baby" to be introduced by him
when he was ready for it, thus allowing him in the sessions to
feel in charge and letting myself be the helpless child. And, indeed, many sessions were spent by him reading one schoolbook
after the other, making me feel totally useless, controlled, and
shut off, like the baby inside himself to which, as yet, we did
not have access.

When I felt that this stage had lasted long enough, I asked
him one day during a pause in his reading, in which he had appeared particularly threatened by the silence, what he was afraid
would happen to him if he stopped reading. Did he think he
came to the clinic as if it were a school, or why, did he think,
was he coming to see me? For a while he did not answer; but
soon afterwards, dropping his book, he began, in a very hyperactive manner, to go around the room, touching everything,
opening drawers, and dashing about at such a speed that it paralyzed me. Meanwhile, he was flooding me with all sorts of questions. These, too, shot out of his mouth at such a speed that
it was obvious to me that they did not want an answer: "Do you
live here, do you sleep on that bed?" Then, touching something
on my desk, "Can I take it home? What is this? Can I have it?"
His behavior was escalating into a frenzy of activities, questions,
and excitement, which suddenly filled up the whole room, and
I felt their aim was to render me impotent, as there was no room
or gap for me to say anything at all. All I could have done was
to take up and exert a controlling stance, like a superego authority, and this I did not want to do. Now that the "big-man" mask
had been dropped, I was beginning to see the chaotic baby and
his terrifying confusion, resulting, I felt, from his persecutory
shame and guilt. The interesting feature of the shift was its au-
tomatic swing from one position to its opposite without any in-
between stage or transition time. He took me by surprise, and

I began to understand what the difficulties must have been like at home. It also gave me an idea of how much he had felt that things happened to him and that things suddenly changed, finding him totally baffled and unprepared — as I had found myself in the countertransference. This led me to speculate on his weaning, and how his mother's departure must have occurred very suddenly, without any explanations to him and without allowing him time to adjust to the situation.

The following session was the one in which the "big mess" took place. Ricky rushed into the therapy room, again carrying a book in his hand, and, without a word, he checked that everything was in order. Then he began to read. I said that he was starting to read again to avoid getting out of control, as had happened on the previous occasion, because I might tell him off. His face looked much more relaxed than in previous interviews. He dropped the book and moved to the table, where pencil, paint, and paper were displayed, and said, "I want to do a proper painting." He sat down at the little table in front of a large sheet of paper and, as I was pouring out some water from the tap into a pot for his brush, he started painting a square with large strokes of dark, blackish paint. While mixing the paint with the brush in the pot, he was becoming excited. "I am drawing a house," he explained. "It is a black-and-white house." As he was struck by the contrast of the black and white lines, he said, "No, it is grey," smearing the colors one into the other and adding more colors while naming them.

While asking questions, Ricky had begun to show his manic hyperactive behavior of the previous day by pouring out all the paint from each individual pot onto the paper. He looked at me defiantly and said, "I need more water and more paint." This continued until a thick, slimy mess had covered the paper and was beginning to flow from the paper onto the table and down to the floor. He was looking increasingly anxious. He went to the tap and busied himself with filling up the pots and pouring out the water from one into the other, mixing into it all the paint left over. Then, taking the brushes and sprinkling water all over the place, he said, half defiantly and half fearfully, "They are having a wee." He then filled up the pots and poured water direct- ly onto the painting, until the water became a puddle on the floor. Then very anxiously he ran to the table, trying, with both arms spread around the little table, to prevent the water from overflowing onto the floor. In a very peremptory way he ordered me, "Stop that tap." "You are asking me to help you to stop the uncontrollable mess you feel is pouring from inside you, which is making you feel very anxious and frightened," I said.

This interpretation shifted Ricky's behavior to the defensive. He was suddenly a "big man" again. Very competently he asked me for a wiping cloth, said the painting was too soggy, and threw it away. Then he wiped his hands clean, rushed to where the toys were placed, and began to play with some little cars, taking a family car and attaching a small trailer to it. All the time he had been very curious about the contents of my big cupboard, giving it inquisitive glances. Then suddenly he rushed to the cupboard in which the toy boxes of my other patients were kept, cpened it wide, climbed into it, and tried to get hold of one of the toy boxes. I said he wanted to have everything inside the room and inside the cupboard.

Realizing that he could not have things his own way, Ricky said, reaching for the door handle, "I am going to my daddy," and waited to see my reaction. "You want to go back to your good daddy," I said, "as I have now become a bad person by not letting you have what you want." He smacked my hand and stepped back from the door he had opened. I closed it, and as I was saying that he had smacked my hand as he had got very angry with me, he sat back very stiffly on his chair and started reading his schoolbook aloud to himself. The story was about Janet and John helping mother to make cakes. He changed the words of the story and angrily read aloud: "You make horrible cakes." "You feel I am a horrible mummy," I added, "and you want to go back to your good daddy, as I deserve to be left by you for being so horrible." He took some small pieces of paper from his desk, wrote on them, and hid them under the telephone on my desk, ordering me: "I want to find them still there when I come back next time, but I will not write my telephone number on them as you are horrible and should not ring me up!" Having said that, he made a little drawing on another piece of paper, which, he said, was a nice present for me; he then offered to fix up my drawer, which, he said, was broken. I commented that he had attacked me and smacked me when he had felt I was being horrible to him, but now he also wanted to please me and to repair the damage he had done, as he felt he had made me into a "broken-up mummy." This reference to a "broken-up mummy" unleashed his persecutory guilt and anger, and once again he attacked me and turned the room upside-down in a sort of manic frenzy, running about in the midst of a great deal of disorganized, scattered, and broken-up talk and activity, in the grip of persecutory anxieties of the sort stirred up by archetypal fantasies of the bad mother-breast, resulting from his aggressive impulses and destructive wishes against the frustrating breast reexperienced in the transference.

In the first interview, the father and the stepmother had heavily projected all the badness onto the mother who had left, confusing their own personal infantile unresolved problems with the reality of Ricky's situation. There had been a lot of hatred and resentfulness on the part of the father toward his ex-wife, which he also attributed to Ricky. In fact, I found out from the boy that he thought he himself was bad, and that it was his bad messiness that had made his good inner and outer mother abandon him, as, in his view, she had left in order to punish him. It was his misery and guilt that induced his "bad," regressive behavior, as he could not forgive himself and did not want anybody else to forgive him either. His superego was quite merciless.

It was only through the work we did together, and through his becoming aware of his own infantile fantasies as something distinct, no matter how similar to real events they appeared to be, that Ricky was able to feel "good" again. For this to take place, the influence of the destructive collective shadow projection within the family had to be put into the right perspective; thus both his own archetypal fantasies and those of his parents had to be sorted out, so that the relationship, both internal and external, with his mother and his love for her could once again come to the fore and be reestablished. Only this could make reparation possible, and make forgiveness of her and of himself take place; but for this to happen he needed the analytic space, and me in it, making a space inside myself to let him be and feel each time as he really felt, protected from collective archetypal shadow projections. It was my awareness of his need for such space—which Winnicott defines as the state of being alone in the presence of mother—and my analytic sensitivity that made me hold back from making, in the beginning, some obvious, stock interpretation, waiting instead until I felt in touch and in tune with what he was to bring me in the sessions. In this way, by not competing with him and knowing better, I avoided humiliating him with my "knowledge," and I reduced his comprehension and consequent shameful feelings.

If I omitted to stress first his able and competent side, Ricky became easily persecuted in his sessions by comments pointing to his baby side. Any hint about his messy side shamed him and tended to make him "become" rather than feel totally helpless and incompetent and "incontinent," which immediately produced a defensive, all-knowing, omnipotent, false reaction. When he experienced excessive persecution and guilt in the sessions, his ego tended to splinter, and at these points he would generally become excited and physically hyperactive. In such moments interpretative work became totally impossible, and I experienced him as a very disturbed and difficult patient.

When Ricky exhibited his grown-up adult-like behavior, on the other hand, his own control of the baby within was so strict that again I felt he was unreachable. Because he could not come for intensive analysis, I had to be very aware and perceptive of his level of tolerance of frustration and distress during the sessions and between them, in order that the treatment should not break down. Thus I had to devise a method of responding and almost anticipating his sudden shifts between opposites in order to keep him in the center (ego) area, where the therapeutic alliance could take place, and to phrase the interpretations in such a way as always to bring together the "good" and the "bad" sides — in his case the big and the small — in order to avoid eliciting manic flights and unbearable persecutions in him, both on the part of the archetypal images of the "superman" and of the "messy devalued baby" (I am referring to cultural patterns of his environment, where only adults are valued and little children are devalued).

I also had to avoid restraining Ricky's behavior through active interventions, as he would experience this as a controlling hand on my part. I would become the "controlling parent," and he would then defy me to exert more control, with the aim of repeating in the sessions the battles over toilet training that he was fighting with his stepmother at home, and the battles he had fought over going to sleep with his father, when both parents had either been defeated or had had to resort to physical violence in order to make him comply.

Ricky had a great passion for painting, which, as it later emerged, he had inherited from his mother, who had been an art student. He used pots and paint both to express himself and to make diabolical messes, which he always cleaned up in a very agitated and compulsive way. The messes always began, as in the first interview, by colors being mixed together and water added to them, which made the mixture unmanageable. The mixing of colors and the brushes and paint pots seemed to represent primal scene fantasies that could be analyzed through his therapy.

What emerged in his treatment was his need to develop a containing boundary around the baby and his mess, in which he could feel safe to express himself — that is, to assimilate his "baby shadow." He worked hard at it by himself, making the best he could of my comments, interpretations, and presence, but it was clear that he was building his own inner frame within the sessions, which he experienced as a container holding the whole of him together. This feature was manifested in the way he asked questions for which he did not want any answers, while he wanted me there, and by a game he played at building frames. He was a very determined, intelligent, and humorous child, and I felt at later stages that his sense of humor helped me to put his behavior into perspective for him, which meant he could then have a good joke about himself and his siblings and the way they would "gang up and drive daddy and mummy mad," or he could joke and pull my leg in the session and enjoy being "a funny clown" and making fun of himself, making a mess, being unable to do something, or talking "baby talk," which was not so threatening for him. He could allow himself to be muddled, foolish, not-knowing, and little, and not worry too much as he came to accept both his sides. He could now feel more often like a baby, loved and appreciated by mother—both by his inner one and his real mother outside—rather than like an abandoned, messy, and unwanted baby who had to delude himself, to be "grown-up" in order to feel loved.

The gap between the child's subjective needs and the mother's empathic response to them leads the growing child gradually to experience the negative side of the dependency, which evokes in him feelings of impotence and helplessness in degrees that vary according to the inner resources of the child on the one hand, and the maternal capacities of the mother on the other.

Frustration generated by this state of affairs can be made more tolerable for the baby by omnipotent fantasies of self-fulfillment, and by splitting his frustrating object into a good one and a bad one, retaining the good and pushing the bad one away.

While too much separation from the mother at the beginning of life endangers life itself, this becomes less extreme as the child grows up. At the same time, the acquisition of a more realistic perception of himself and of his abilities in relation to those of his mother prompts in the small child feelings of inadequacy, guilt, and shame, along with feelings of guilt and shame about that inadequacy and smallness, and envy of the powerful resources of the mother and father, which he fears he will never be able to acquire. The sensitivity of the parents to such anxiety and fear in their child enables them to facilitate the child's task of integrating his inadequacies without his feeling compelled to disown them.

REFERENCES

Bion, W. (1962). *Learning from Experience.* New York: Basic Books.

Grotstein, J. (1985). "A Proposed Revision for the Psychoanalytic Concept of Death Instincts." *Yearbook of Psychoanalysis and Psychotherapy,* Vol. 1, pp. 239-326. New Jersey: Concept Press.

Hultberg, P. (1988). "Shame: A Hidden Emotion." *J. Analyt Psychol.,* 33, 2.

Jung, C. G. (1951). "The Shadow." *Coll. Wks. 9, 2.*

Miller, S. (1986). *The Experience of Shame.* London: The Analytic Press.

Ogden, T. (1986). *The Matrix of the Mind.* New York: Jason Aronson.

Chapter 6

THE VALUE OF REGRESSION IN CHILD ANALYSIS

Regression is usually understood by the layman as a movement backwards into earlier states of being and behaving; it is often feared and considered less valuable than progression, which is seen as moving forward in a positive way in the direction of maturity and growth. While one cannot deny that this view carries some truth with regard to patients who enter analysis, regression, both spontaneous and induced by the setting, constitutes an important phase of the treatment, without which further development cannot and will not take place. Adolescence has to be considered separately as a stage of life in which conflicts based on regression/progression dynamics constitute the core of the therapy.

Jung describes psychic dynamic systems as developing along elliptic spirals rather than linear movements. Thus in the course of the process of growth and individuation, regression and progression seem to alternate according to the level in the spiral reached by the individual. Jung often wrote of the need for an individual to "regress in order to progress"— *reculer pour mieux sauter*. According to Jung, by delving into the unconscious, one could discover shadow elements and new potentialities that had become split off during the course of one's development, and by the process of "working them through" with an analyst one could manage to integrate them. He quoted examples from initiation practices and rituals in different cultures through the centuries, and one could say that the practice of psychoanalysis and analytical psychology is based on such models.

Freud stressed the value of regression in analysis to earlier stages of ego development (we would see this as taking place in the realm of the personal unconscious). While not denying the importance of Freud's discoveries, Jung emphasized the natural healing powers of the psyche, which could be set in motion both by cultural religious rituals and by analytical or mystical experiences, because of certain basic structures he had discovered in the depths of the psyche, which he termed the "archetypes" and the "self." He defined the self as the totality of the personality and, paradoxically, also its center, within which the ego develops according to rhythms initiated by the self. According to Jung, in cases where the ego has become over-defended and too inflexible, causing psychic imbalance, a realignment of the ego/self axis can be brought about by his method of analysis, which aimed at helping the patient to focus his attention on his inner world and on the events taking place there, and to reflect on how his personal myth had become constellated in the unconscious.

On the basis of his interest in children and his long experience of working with them, Fordham applied Jung's concepts to the earliest stages of life.

In thinking about regression, one can say that it has therapeutic effects because "through" regression damaged parts of the self can be reached, identified, understood and relived in token form (Fordham, 1978). When discussing the function and value of regression, Jung wrote:

> The regressive tendency only means that the patient is seek-

ing himself in his childhood memories sometimes for better, sometimes for worse. His development was onesided; it left important items of character and personality behind and thus ended in failure. That is why he has to go back. (Jung, 1930, p. 33)

This statement is valid for both adults and children alike. Because the damaged parts of the personality in both cases can lie in the infant part of the patient, regression to infantile states needs to take place for a healthy development to be released. Conceiving the self as a dynamic system that deintegrates and reintegrates rhythmically is useful for understanding how regression can take place — in fact, the dynamic system of the self leads either through regression to the original self, or through progression to the realization that the same object can be good and bad (Fordham, 1973).

This view takes us far from the simplistic concept of progression and regression on a linear model. The deintegrative (opening-up) phase leads to an integrative (closing-up) phase, which reestablishes the integrated state of the self until a new deintegration needs to occur, and so on, in rhythmic sequence. We could say that each regressive phase is a deintegration leading to a progressive phase, an integration, where a new element — or deintegrate — is being assimilated in a phasic movement suggested by Jung's view of the spiral. However, both Jung and Fordham acknowledge that in certain cases the smooth functioning of the psychic dynamics cannot take place, and disturbances occur. Jung attributes most of the disturbances to a splitting off by the ego of unconscious elements. A rigid ego, which needs to be in control and uses rigid defences to keep the unconscious elements at bay, can lead the personality to serious mental illness. An inflation, a breakdown, or *dis*integration of the mental structure may be the psychic danger lurking in the background. According to Fordham's model, damage can occur when deintegration leads to disintegration — hence to psychotic confusional states — rather than to reintegration. Fordham also postulates the possibility of faulty functioning in the primary self, and this would account for infantile autism. A primary self that is unable to deintegrate would allow only minimal integration to take place in the ego.

This model of mental dynamics is useful in writing about regression because it is flexible and accounts for the constant alternation of regressed and integrated states, which can take place many times in the individual psyche in the course of one day (shifts between day and night, wakefulness and sleep). The deintegrative-reintegrative sequences occur with greater intensity and frequency at certain stages of one's life—as when, for instance, sudden important events that need to be processed by the unconscious and assimilated by consciousness occur both internally and externally. The deintegrative, regressive phase can be experienced as regression into sleep, physical illness, or temporary mental illness, eating binges, confusional states, and depression. Such states then move on to the integrative, progressive phases. Pathological depression, however, can be considered a failure of the ego to deintegrate. One could say that the deintegrative process gets stuck for lack of psychic energy, which is deployed in keeping the aggressive elements split off. However, if because of severe lack of flexibility the ego fights the deintegrative tendency of letting go in order to regress, then eventually, once the regression has occurred, one will notice the upsurge of an inflationary tendency to compensate for and contain unbearable anxieties, as in the following case. In instances of psychotic disintegration, the ego does not succeed in coming together again, because the intensity of the energy explosion seems to splinter and shatter the ego beyond repair.

In extreme forms of regression to non-ego states—such as the very early states of infancy—verbal analysis is no longer possible, as there is no patient there for the analyst to address himself to. This situation points to the fact that an infantile state of delusion of fusion (mouth and breast felt as one by the baby) has been reached in the transference, and the analyst will have to endure the situation, holding it and allowing the patient to create in the present the illusion of fusion with the breast, which seemed to have been missing in his early infancy, and out of which a good reintegration can hopefully occur. This state of affairs is discussed in the case of a psychotic boy for whom each deintegration turned into an explosive disintegration, which shattered his ego; no integrative motion could be fostered by my verbal interpretation, but I felt that my presence and physical care — like a mother — was what was required by the patient. Working with adults, one is often faced with a great resistance to regression (use of the couch, references to childhood), as in the case of a patient who stated that he had come to me because he thought I was a Jungian, and he was expecting to talk about highly spiritual issues. As I worked away at interpreting his grandiose archetypal dreams in relation to his childhood fantasies, he became very resentful, and, accusing me with great hositility of "being a Freudian," he threatened to walk out of the session. As it later emerged, this young man, a former heroin addict, was terrified of regression, which his ego equated to a malignant dependency similar to the effect of the drug. He feared that this would develop in the analysis, and he had to fight it with all his strength. His addiction had in fact placed an experience of dependence on an "ideal" breast, as due to a separation at birth from his mother he had not managed to bond with her.

With small children, however, the situation is different, as in them the wish to grow up is very strong and (due to the reality of the situation) militates against their regressive tendencies. Besides, through play they are allowed to shift more freely than adults from regressive tendencies to the wish to grow up, and they are able to try out both roles (child and parent).

Examples of regression occurred during the analysis of four children of different ages, presenting different pathologies, and requiring different ways of dealing with the regression. Each child regressed according to his personal mode — Robert by somatizing, Ricky by disintegrating and becoming manic for brief spells.

David, whose thinking regressed into acting whenever the analyst touched on any of his vulnerable areas, would revert to omnipotent defences and grandiose identification with godlike figures. John, whose hardly existing ego used to melt away at the slightest frustration in his sessions, regressed totally into the original self.

Robert

Robert (see chapter 2), was three years old when he was brought to me; he had been referred because he refused to separate from his mother and attend a playgroup. He had developed various phobias, tantrums, nightmares, and clinging behavior at the stage of separation from the mother. He was an intelligent, verbal child, the elder of two boys (his brother was only a year younger) — the first live child born to a mother with a history of miscarriages. He was born two months prematurely and spent his first two weeks of life seriously ill in an incubator.

Robert settled into analysis after some initial difficulties and was able to communicate well with me. Although he left the mother fairly quickly and came to play in the room with me, at times of distress he would run out and hide, crying, in his mother's arms and would only return if she came too. He found transference interpretations distressing and wanted his mother in the room as a protection from them. My being able to stand his pain and panic in a calm but concerned way, sharing his distress without giving in to the wish to comfort him, slowly enabled him to manage these difficult times without mother there. I understood these states as a reliving of his infantile experiences in the incubator, but I never mentioned this to him in that way. This phase of the analysis, when he constantly called his mother into the room, lasted about three-and-a-half months.

In the second phase, when Robert was mostly accompanied by his father, primal scene fantasies began to surface in the material. My interpretation of them in the transference made him extremely anxious and aroused in him feelings of despair. If his mother was waiting for him, he would at once run out into her arms, where he would cry inconsolably, regressing to the baby-in-arms state. He used regression as a defence and flight from the ambivalence of conflicting emotions in the session. At one point, after one session in which he had exhibited a very strong ambivalence, he missed the next four sessions, as he developed bad bronchitis. The bronchitis and the respiratory tract infection were very severe, so that his analysis became irregular. I had to make the mother and father understand that it might have something to do with a "reaction" to the treatment, and that it would be helpful if they could bring him to see me as often as possible during his illness. I understood his somatization both as a regression to his babyhood, to his early period in the incubator, and as a way of dealing with his rage in a manner his parents could understand, and for which they would comfort him and so remove him from my presence, which was making him feel bad. The whole family was prone to somatization.

Following Robert's illness, I had to be absent for a week. During the weeks that followed, we had to work through a great deal of negative feeling and violent impulses, such as his wanting to shoot or bite me, and, occasionally, actually hitting me. After I had verbalized his feelings and impulses toward me, he was able to accept them and link them up with his feeling that I had abandoned him, as he thought his mother had done when his baby brother was born, and as he imagined that I too had gone away to attend to my own baby; he became much more loving, and it seemed as if he was going to be my friend again. He appeared to have begun surfacing from the massive regression of the previous weeks. At one point he started coughing, and he coughed for a long time. As he looked particularly miserable, I commented on it. He said that he seemed to have had this cough for a very long time now, and he expressed his view that he felt the doctor was not helping him. As soon as I added that he felt I was not helping him either, he began to feel less uncomfortable and angry with his cough and went back to playing. It seemed to me that from his experience of having been separated from me and the following misery, and from my interpreting it and linking it up with his baby self, he was beginning to acquire an idea about us being separate beings, and that he could not control my comings and goings, but he could now begin to trust that I would come back. The regression was definitely beginning to give way to a reintegration, as we were able to observe during the following week, when the cough at last began to improve. It eventually disappeared as he developed a game of looking after an imaginary baby horse called Tracey, who, he said, was born at the time he started his treatment. He said that the horse had a cough now, and using the furniture in the room he built what looked like an incubator—a womb-like warm place, where she had to be put to sleep and kept very warm by him until she recovered.

This massive deintegration, brought about by the deep regression, was the blocking factor that prevented Robert from separating from his mother in a way appropriate for his age, and so get on with his life. In this case, the boy's ego was healthy enough, and once the stumbling block had been removed, his growth processes could carry on in all areas of his personality.

Ricky

Ricky (see chapter 5) was five years old when he was brought to see me on account of his aggressive, destructive behavior both at school and at home. He did not find it difficult to stay in the room with me as long as he did not feel threatened by some comment of mine relating to his feelings about his mother's departure and his guilt about it. It was here that he seemed confused, muddled, and in a mess about himself and the world around him.

For quite a number of sessions Ricky managed to cope, sticking to an adhesive identification with a "big person" and reading to me most of the time. When he eventually relinquished the "big-man mask," a "mess" took place in the room, yet it was still an "actual" mess, which stood for the emotional one inside him. This happened as soon as he began to paint; his manic hyperactive behavior of the previous day would surface again. Mixing paint and water excited him, and the excitement was difficult to contain. He at first struggled with a wish to mess my room — me — up, and with the fear that I would punish him for his bad wish; this he defiantly turned into action and created a proper mess on his little table. As this was happening, he was also struggling with his wish to contain it, regain ego control, or flood the room, letting the unconscious, chaotic, infantile feelings take over. He expressed this conflict when, in a peremptory tone of voice, he ordered me to stop the tap. Instead of acting as he wished me to and thus satisfy his wish, I responded by verbalizing that he wanted me to stop the uncontrollable mess that seemed to be inside him from pouring out and drowning us both.

The exclusively verbal intervention on my part had a twofold aim: to make sense of what he was feeling but also to frustrate his omnipotent fantasies, thus inducing a deintegrating regression.

So far the mess that Ricky was displaying was still a concrete one outside him, and he was clearly fighting inside himself the chaotic emotions that my interpretations were stirring up. Once again he tried the identification with a big daddy person, and he tidied up and cleaned up. But this did not last long, as some of what I had said had got inside him and was working as a disturbance to his usual defensive system. He then tried to adopt manic flight and began to run around the room and out of it, which I verbalized to him as his attempt to leave me — the bad mummy who frustrated him — to go to his good daddy. He reacted by attacking me and saying I was horrible. Following his physical attack on me, I commented that he felt he had made me into a broken-up mummy. This reference to a "broken-up" mummy penetrated deep inside him and stirred up all his feelings of guilt and persecution and rage. He literally went to pieces, attacked me again, and turned the room upside-down in a sort of manic frenzy. He ran about, with much disorganized, scattered, and broken-up chatter and activity, in the grip of persecutory anxieties of the kind stirred up by archetypal fantasies of the bad mother-breast, resulting from his aggressive impulses and destructive wishes against the frustrating breast, and reexperienced in the transference. This state of affairs lasted for a good fifteen minutes, until he slowly regained some level of integration.

It seems clear to me that earlier on he had been struggling to regain control, and he had stopped the deintegrative move because his ego was terrified of becoming overwhelmed (disintegrated). The upsurge of emotions fostered by my interpretation, however, broke through his defensive barrier, and his organizing ego defences went to pieces. He experienced here and now the very deintegration that he feared, which gave way to a reintegration by the end of the session, thanks to the analyst's holding and care.

This was the pattern of Ricky's therapy, and one could say in conclusion that Ricky had been afraid of letting go because, in the absence of his mother (earlier on in his life), he had already suffered a major disintegration.

David

David was a ten-year-old boy, seen in analysis four times per week by Mr. Ian Williamson (to whom I am indebted for permission to use this material). He was attending a day unit, as his behavior had proven uncontrollable at school and at home, where he had exhibited great violence and extreme learning difficulties. His emotional disturbance appeared very severe, and he was diagnosed as borderline.

David was a twin. His mother had been very depressed after the birth of the twins, as the husband had had a breakdown and had been unable to support her and the babies. Eventually he left home to be admitted to a mental hospital. David seemed to have developed an immediate and powerful transference to his analyst — in fact, his deintegrations, which at the start of the analysis turned into an explosive disintegration, tended to occur as soon as he caught sight of the analyst coming to him on the way to the therapy room. Thus, by the time he entered the room and the session could begin, he was already well on the way to disintegration.

David's behavior in analysis was characterized by sudden massive regressions, bringing about extreme feelings of helplessness, which he tried to escape by massive acting-out and/or fantasies of inflated omnipotence.

The following took place in the tenth session of his analysis and is a very typical example of what was going on in his analysis at that time.

As he entered the therapy room, David quickly rearranged the furniture and went into an elaborate game of being Superman, jumping from the cupboard onto rearranged cushions. He interrupted his game to go to the toilet; on the way back he kicked the other therapy room door. He showed the analyst his new T-shirt, which, he said, his teacher had given him. He ordered the analyst to rearrange the cushions again and continued to jump from the cupboards onto the cushions. He chattered to himself in a voice the analyst could not understand. He wrapped a blanket around himself and shouted "Superman!" at the top of his voice.

He noticed the other cupboard top in the far corner of the room and rearranged things in a similar manner; however, the shelf was too thin, and David could not get onto it. He became frustrated by this and consequently more manic. He decided he wanted to make a secret camp, and with the analyst's help he managed to push the drawers into the corner. He climbed inside and ordered the analyst to put cushions and the blanket over the top. Eventually he was completely enclosed in the camp. He stayed there in silence. The analyst began to comment; David said, "No words." A few minutes later he emerged, to repeat the

Superman maneuver. He got back into the camp, and there was
silence again. Suddenly he kicked away the sofa cover (which
in his play represented the door) and revealed himself; he lay
in a ball, his head resting on a cushion, his thumb in his mouth.
He looked at the analyst with wistful eyes. He stayed like this
for several minutes before crawling out.

An important development took place for the first time in this
session, as David, having acted out Superman in a manic frenzy, built a camp and went inside this dark, containing, womb-
like place, regressing to the infant state and sucking his thumb.
At last he had felt safe enough in a session to be able to show
to his analyst — if only for a very short spell — his vulnerable soft
baby inside. From that moment onwards, although the omnipotent defences reappeared almost immediately, the baby part,
which he had found in the analysis, was there for him and his
analyst to work with. David had reached through regression "the
damaged part of himself" (Fordham, 1978), and he was going
to be able to make sense of it with the help of his analyst in
the transference.

However, many months of intense work were still required for
David not to need to revert to his omnipotent stunts and violent acts when feeling threatened. During the following session
David marched around the room, unable to settle. The analyst
commented: "I wonder what you're thinking about, David?"

There was no reply. He pulled out his drawer and slammed
it shut. David did the same with his desk drawer. He became
increasingly aggressive and angry. He looked at the analyst
through screwed-up eyes and talked, or rather mumbled, in an
animal-like voice.

The analyst said: "When you're feeling like this, you find it
hard to find words."

David ignored this and made an effort to repeat his stuntman
maneuver (which involved climbing into the top of the cupboard
and jumping down). He made one successful jump. His next
effort led to a hurt ankle.

The analyst asked if he was OK, and then said that he liked to pretend to be a stuntman because he could climb up and escape from the baby David that hurt inside.

David climbed up the cupboard and sat on top, beginning to speak about a god that ruined his life. It affected him here (pointing to his heart). He said it had a long nose and looked like Prince Charles. He then enacted what he called fights with the God, using the cushions.

Here, David revealed to his analyst his fear of an archetypal collective unconscious content that invaded his consciousness. It then became clear that the violence displayed by David was his way to combat the persecuting god that he projected onto the analyst and onto whoever represented a potential danger. He lived in a state of constant persecutory anxieties.

John

This final case is of "John," a psychotic boy (see chapter 7) whose ego suffered such powerful disintegration at the onset of any frustrating circumstance that hardly any analytic integrative work could take place in the three years during which I saw him four times weekly. Most of the time he was unable to play and could only act destructively in the session, attacking the objects in the room physically and me verbally. But when the violence gave way to a regression, he could show me his distress and pain, lying for session after session sucking his thumb, shivering and feeling cold, curled up like a fetus (see Tustin, 1986). His pain was even more unbearable to share than his violence, and difficult to get hold of. When it displayed itself, I seemed to be left alone in the room with his inhuman pain because John's ego had melted away. During those periods I had to nurse him, cover him up with a blanket, and talk to him as I would to a tiny baby; he did not know the meaning of my words, and it was the sound of my calm voice that he found comforting. Both his extreme aggression, linked to his fantasized omnipotence, and his massive depression, linked to his feelings of total helplessness, were very distressing for me to share, as both states had a dimension greater than life.

During this period John spent hours playing with slime — passing it between his fingers, looking at its shapelessness, and enjoying it sensually. He appeared to get lost in all sorts of sensations, and his play had a repetitive, monotonous quality and a mindlessness that I found difficult to endure. His play then developed in water games. Water would fill up the sink, and he tried to make it flood the room, filling up all the space and overflowing the boundaries in the sink. He fantasized about drowning me and himself in it; thus we would merge, but in merging we would be destroyed.

John appeared to fight the agony of the awareness of separatedness in very extreme ways: by destroying the object because of his unbearable badness, or by melting away himself — that is, destroying his precarious ego consciousness. In this case, due to the extreme explosive quality and fragility of his ego in the face of any frustration that disturbed his delusion of fusion with his object, the integrative process could not take place, because each deintegration produced a succession of explosive disintegration. Therefore in his analysis the regression progression (deintegration-reintegration) rhythm could not be established.

REFERENCES

Fordham, M. (1985). *Exploration into the Self*. L.A.P., Vol. 7. London: H. Karnac Books.

Fordham, M. (1978). *Jungian Psychotherapy*. Chichester: John Wiley.

Fordham, M. (1973). "The Importance of Analysing Childhood for the Assimilation of the Shadow." In *Analytical Psychology: A Modern Science*. L.A.P. London: H. Karnac Books.

Jung, C. G. (1930/54). 154 *The Practice of Psychotherapy*. Coll. Wks. 16, p.33.

Tustin, F. (1986). *Autistic Barriers in Neurotic Patients*. London: H. Karnac Books.

CHAPTER 7

DISORDERS OF THE SELF IN PSYCHOTIC STATES: THE CASE OF AN ELEVEN-YEAR-OLD BOY

Jung, in his studies on the aetiology of schizophrenia in adult patients, came to consider the psychotic seizure as archetypal, concerned with the archetype of the shadow. Such instances he called "acting out," "living the shadow." According to him these patients presented the doctor with a disorder that he classed as a "disorder of the self"; this, he found, occurred in certain personality structures, and he suggested that the destructive process in schizophrenia might be "a mistaken biological defence reaction." He also conceived the delusional systems of schizophrenic patients as an unsuccessful subjective attempt on the part of the patient's self to heal splits and aim for psychological integration. In that way he was the first to see an heuristic value in delusional systems. He also suggested that biochemical changes might play an aetiological part in schizophrenic disorders of the self:

> . . . up to a certain point psychology is indispensable in explaining the nature and causes of the initial emotions which give rise to the metabolic alterations. These emotions seem

to be accompanied by chemical changes that cause specific temporary, or chronic disturbances or lesions. (Jung, 1958)

Following Jung, analytical psychologists have also stressed the purposive defensive function of both acting out and the delusional transference and their potential for healthy development, a way of "living out the shadow," which, through analysis, may lead to integration.

Fordham, in "Notes on Transference," defines acting out "as a special form of defensive behavior based on a projection to which neither analyst nor patient have been able to gain access" (Edwards, 1978; Fordham, 1970; Stein, 1967). Furthermore, Fordham has expanded Jung's self theory by developing the hypothesis of a primal self, thus extending Jung's hypothesis to include the individual's first stage in life. The baby at birth is a psychosomatic unit or "primal self." In his book, *The Self and Autism*, Fordham classes childhood psychosis as a disorder of the primal self and states that

> A healthy infant is primarily a psychosomatic unit or a self, which will contribute by deintegration to [the development of] all psychic structures as they differentiate in the course of growth. . . . idiopathic autism is a disordered state of integration, owing its persistence to the failure of the self to deintegrate. (Fordham, 1976, p. 88)

Deintegration is conceived of as an activity both psychic and physiological—thus corresonding with Jung's view—and localized at the archetypal "red end of the spectrum." I have found his conceptualization of "self and not-self objects" very helpful in clinical work with Jim, a preadolescent patient of mine.

In "Exploration of the Self," Fordham (1985) writes:

> Whether in an adult or in a baby, any object perceived is composite. It is not only a record of what is outside there but is also contributed to by a part of self which is put into it, to give it meaning. When the object is mainly a record of reality, it may be called a reality object; when it is mainly construct-

ed by the self and so records states of the self, made out of extroceptive and introceptive sense data, then it may be called a self object. . . . It was assumed among analytical psychologists that a baby's perception was predominately through self objects and that he lived in a sort of mythological world. That is a very misleading account of infancy. If, however, a sliding scale is envisaged (real object — self-object), then one can study observations in that light. . . . It appears that self objects increase in affectively charged states, whilst in quiet contemplative exploring activities real objects prevail.

A "self-object," according to this definition, would be the only possible one in highly emotionally charged states, and some babies might be relentlessly in the grip of extremely unmodified instinctual drives, which give the whole world a self-object connotation. Anything else is experienced as "not-self," threatening the very survival of the self. In his paper, "Introducing Notself," Stein postulated the existence of a defensive system designed to preserve individual identity. This hypothesis he drew from immunology and from the theory that immunological reactions provide an analogy that usefully shows the psyche annihilates not-self objects. (Stein, 1967)

In childhood autism and other pathological cases, when the focus is placed on "not-self objects" as a danger and a threat and these prevail due to too much affectivity impinging on the baby's self-integrity, these not-self objects develop into persecuting, life-threatening entities that need destroying.

In such a situation there is an overreaction, and eventually all objects are experienced as not-self and attacked or neutralized. Thus little or no inner world can develop, symbolization is hampered, and thought is destroyed.

Another interesting theory on the development of child psychosis has been suggested by Frances Tustin (1981) in her paper, "Autistic Objects." She postulates that at the root of pathological autism lies a basic catastrophe in the relation between the baby and the breast mother, which we as Jungians would call a failure of the self to deintegrate. Her postulate is,

I think, relevant in the case of Jim, as is Bion's theory of the explosive personality and the "creation of mental space."

Jim, a boy of eleven, was referred to me for analysis after a series of hopeless attempts on the part of both parents and the community had failed to bring his destructive violence at the onset of any frustration — within acceptable bounds. By the age of three he had already destroyed a couple of playgroups, and when he moved to school, he continued being outwardly destructive of material objects and aggressive with teachers and school friends. When he was eight, referral to a special boarding school was felt to be necessary. At boarding school he continued to be extremely violent toward staff and children and developed suicidal wishes and fantasies. He made a minor suicide attempt and was eventually removed from school altogether and returned to the parental home. Jim was kept at home by his mother, who, by the time she brought him to me, could no longer cope with him. At home the situation with Jim had been no easier than at school. He was the first of two children. His sister, two years and two months younger, caused no problems and was described by the parents as a rewarding and well-adjusted child, in spite of the burden of having to cope with, and defend herself from, the aggressive, jealous behavior of her brother.

Jim had been a problem child from the very beginning, although no physical cause had been diagnosed. He had been a restless and fretful baby, crying all the time from birth onwards, and was constantly on tranquilizers. His mother felt that she could not soothe him or comfort him in her arms as he had not been a cuddly baby; but he had been easy to feed and had found his thumb very early.

When the parents came to see me, they both sounded hopeless about the situation with Jim. The hostility and murderousness that I sensed in the parents against both Jim and potential helpers was great, although disguised, especially in the mother, by an irritatingly polite and kind manner. The father was ashamed of Jim's lack of achievement and genuinely worried about Jim and his future. He seemed to be the only person who could control Jim's aggression, at times by violence, and who did not seem too worried by it. It was his nonachieving at school that frightened and shamed him most. It soon emerged that he, too, was a violent man, and that he had had a psychotic break-down two years previously and was still receiving medication from a psychiatrist.

The mother, on the other hand, described Jim's violence as frightening and causing her utmost difficulties, as she was to-tally unable to control or manage it. Jim seemed to play sadistic games with her all the time, in which he was always the aggres-sor and she the meek victim, at least until the father returned home. Then she complained to him and seemed to use him un-consciously to get her revenge against Jim, who, in turn, became the victim, while she, having obtained her revenge, indirectly appeared passive and good. She projected a shadowless image of herself as a sweet, gentle housewife, always immaculately tidy, a good, self-sacrificing mother, never losing her temper in spite of Jim's unbearable provocation. I felt she was a cold person whose real feelings were hard to detect and whose potential rages were unquenchable. Her meekness and whingeing confused Jim and frustrated him no end. His aim in life seemed to be to pro-voke and attack her, to destroy her angelic mask and to reveal, at the cost of his own life, what he seemed to experience as the "stone woman" who lay behind it. I thought that the family dy-namics were clearly psychotic and established within rigid splits between extremes of good and bad, which could not be reconciled.

Jim and his "hopeless, incurable madness" could be used by them as a scapegoat and a recipient for all their bad projections. Unfortunately, Jim found a perverse excitement and a self-destructive pleasure in going along with and provoking these fantasies, both in the family and in the wider world. At times he seemed to convey by his behavior that if he could not be the best, at least he could be "the worst person" in the world. It was the mother who first pointed out to me that Jim was worrying to live with and needed to be strictly monitored, for, as she said, "He would do thoughtless acts, with no regard to consequences." His violent behavior was socially unacceptable and dangerous because he appeared as if possessed by violence and *unable to think*.

Jim's situation at the time he was referred to me had caused serious concern and worry in whoever had been close to him, coupled with the feeling that something needed to be done before the onset of adolescence to prevent the worst from happening during the course of his thoughtless acts, both to himself and to others.

I knew from the start that his treatment, if it was going to take place, would entail massive amounts of acting out and testing of my ability to contain him and to give him solid, strong boundaries. I felt that his tendency to violence and to acting out did not constitute a good prognosis for analysis.

When he came for the first interview, he struck me as a good-looking, chubby, physically fit boy with an attractive face and an open smile, and with a somewhat artifically sophisticated manner. He followed his mother to the waiting room, and I observed that he walked in an unusual way, trailing behind her as if stepping on her shadow. They gave me the impression of being enclosed within the same boundary. It was as if the two of them formed a "whole" and were sharing a private, enclosed psychic area, acting a *folie à deux*. I felt out of touch with them and excluded by both.

Things changed, however, as soon as I was left alone with Jim. He appeared much more able to be separate from his mother than I had assumed. It quickly emerged that we would have to behave in the same symbiotic way, and that my not responding to his demands enraged him furiously and caused his destructive attacks on me and on the material objects in my room. He experienced me as behaving as a "not-self object" unless I participated in his symbiotic fantasy. This puzzled me at first, as his reaction was grossly out of proportion to the cause. His mood shifted automatically, and suddenly his violence was unleashed. What struck me was his total inability to tolerate even the slightest frustration, as shown by an extract from his very first session.

He opened the toy box in the room and was visibly pleased at finding a gun in it. "The best gun I have ever seen," he said. "Can I have it?" he asked, and I told him that it was for him to play with in the room. He asked the same question several times about some of the little cars. So I added that if he meant could he take it away with him, I had said he could not, as the toys were for him to play with here, when he came to see me. He then made all the cars fall down to the ground and, in a deliberate way, smashed them all up. I said that he had smashed them up because he was angry with my refusal to let him take the cars away, as he does at home when his parents will not allow him to do what he wants. "Good guess," he said, and added, "I smash things up to make my parents angry." "Are you going to get angry?" he asked me while throwing the little cars against the wall with increased violence. I felt that the wall was equated in his mind to my "No." It represented for him a concrete, bad obstacle, the "nonself," the "nonfit"— something that was in the way of his wish fulfilment and did not allow him to maintain the delusion of his omnipotence. The rage had to discharge itself, and he attacked it in order to smash it down and to destroy it. Because of his rage, the cars, the wall, and myself had, by now, all the quality of bad not-self objects. When the James Bond car lost its steering wheel, he panicked, looked at me, and said meekly, "I can fix it," and then added that he was good at fixing Lego cars. At this point the affective change seems more intense and for a short spell there is for him a possibility to think about "fixing things" up. The "self-objects" prevailed, as Fordham says, during less charged states, but in Jim's case the dawning in his consciousness of the amount of fixing up which he needed doing created an even greater frustration. Thus he carried on attacking the cars, the wall, and the room, asking me at the same time whether I was going to see him again, and how often. He then pointed a gun to his head and said he was going to kill himself. I replied that he really did not mean to kill himself, but to threaten me with the gun, as I was bad and wicked for not letting him do what he wanted — and, also that he feared I might attack him like he was attacking my toys and my room.

During the following session he asked me whom else I saw, and I interpreted his jealousy in relation to his mother giving her attention to his sister and father. He put a little car into his pocket. I pointed out to him what he was doing, mentioning at the same time his fear that if he did not take it away, I might give it to another child. As a response he threw it out, smashing the car and the rest of the toys against the wall. He looked at me defiantly and asked, "What do you feel about it?" "How do you think I feel?" I replied. "You are sad," he answered. "Yes, because in order to try to anger me you are destroying all the good things I have got for you that you like so much," I answered. He became quiet and thoughtful for a moment. At the end of the session he gave me the little car, or what was left of it, to put back into the toy box. He kissed it better, very gently, and then said, "I like your voice, you speak calmly. I like calm. If the volcano erupted, you would be speaking calmly." He was now completely lost in his fantasy, speaking very softly and holding himself still. "Would that comfort you?" I asked. "Yes." And he added: "What would yo do if the volcano erupted?" Talking to himself, he continued: "I would take my gun, this car, and an action man and wait for it to kill me." Meanwhile I went on to say that it felt at times as if the volcano was inside him. He lifted his head, looked at me very intensely and smiled. He was asking me to help him with that volcano part of himself by using my calm voice to contain it, which, he said, was soothing and reassuring.

That was his first statement asking for help. I realized that his wish for me to stop the volcano's eruption by talking to it would be a mighty enterprise, and I then began to expect and prepare for the great explosion, as those we had had so far were to be considered very minor. But even then I had not realized what I had let myself in for. As we got more and more into the treatment, his violence and aggression increased; not only did he destroy all the toys and attack all the pieces of furniture in the room, but he directed his attacks to the windows, glasses, door knobs, and fireplace, he caused the sink to flood the room, and he climbed — at a dash — to reach an electric fire fixed to the wall well out of his reach, and nearly managed to electrocute himself. But his most violent attacks were against the wall, which, I think, he equated with a boundary or division between him and me. He dug into the wall with any hard object he could use, and when, eventually, in order to prevent further disasters, I limited the room's furniture to soft cushions, he kicked holes in the wall with his shoes and bit into the cushions to get the feathers out.

I realised that it was me as a "brick-wall-breast-mother" that he was out to destroy. My interpretations, geared to reach his very damaged infantile self, were often repeated without any results. He managed to neutralize them, exploding them as flying, bad, attacking objects on a trajectory between me and him before they could actually penetrate his mental space. His way of dealing with my interpretations and comments often reminded me of the game "Space Invaders," on which he was actually very keen. It was the to and fro of communication in space and time that marked and underlined our separateness, and this he experienced as destructive and something he automatically had to destroy.

His outbursts also aimed to destroy his and my thoughts and interpretations, but not my physical self, as he needed me in flesh and blood. He needed my arms, my lap, and my voice to protect and contain him against the bad, persecuting objects whenever he felt them attacking him, as a very small infant needs the mother in flesh and blood to modify and transform archetypal experiences into human ones.

Archetypal images of nonhuman kinds — such as natural forces,

volcanic eruptions, earthquakes, floods, ice, and fire — emerged
in Jim's material in session after session. I speculated that it might
have to do with a faulty functioning of the deintegrative-
reintegrative process in Jim's primal self (Edwards, 1978). The
breast mother and the environment appear to have been experienced by Jim as icy-cold and hostile; thus, instead of the life-
mother and a warm, nourishing breast, he encountered the ice-
cold breast and the death-mother at the time of his birth.

His material was rich in images that could be related to alche-
my, and Jung's study, *Mysterium Coniunctionis* — which inquires
into the separation and synthesis of opposites in the psyche —
is relevant when considering the imagery produced by Jim during his play. The self, according to Jung's definition, is the totality of the conscious and unconscious psyche, of psychic and
somatic, which, he found, were represented in shapes and images of the circle, in mandalas, and, in their simplest form, in
the triangle, or trinity, and the square, or quaternity, represented thus:

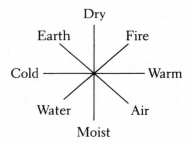

Jung states that the factors that come together in the *coniunctio* are conceived as opposites, either confronting one another
in enmity or attracting one another in love. The above diagram
caught my attention, and it seemed to me that in the case of
Jim the graphic representation might be:

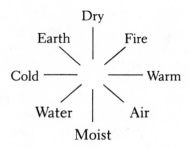

The connecting links between each pair of opposites here are unrelated and disconnected, with a kind of hole in the center where his ego should have been operative, sustaining the pull of the opposites or bringing about their synthesis. In fact, the opposites pulling at a weak ego, as in Jim's case, are very likely to produce a break-down at the point where the intensity of the opposite pull is at its greatest. Thus his sudden loss of ego and subsequent inability to sustain links confused me and also made me unable to think.

In the sessions I often felt that, when all my skills as an analyst were attacked and destroyed so that the only thing I had to fall back on were my instincts, I should follow whatever they suggested to me to be right, because I would not use my thinking or my knowledge, which he attacked and reduced to bits. In his paper, "Attacks on Analysis," Barry Proner describes a similar case of a child who mercilessly attacked his thinking and his ability to create links (Proner, 1983). At one stage I found myself as if in the eye of a tornado attacked by the various objects that Jim frantically threw about at the wall and in the air. It was like being in the midst of a volcanic eruption, at the mercy of the elements let loose in his unconscious, which I had no power whatsoever to control.

Thus I stopped making interpretations and tried strict management; but this did not bring any better results. The fury of the elements that had mounted up in Jim's unconscious was far beyond his, or my, control. It would last as long as it pleased itself;

then, suddenly, the storm would be over, and we could enjoy
some peace. I could then become his analyst once more, until
it all started up again. During each pause we were both usually
completely worn out and exhausted, and he lay flat in a sort of
catatonic state, while I rested, taking a deep breath, dreading
the next storm that would soon be stirred up again in his unconscious, working out in my mind how to delay it, making emer-
gency plans for survival, and trying to imagine it in order to
contain it in my mind.

Whenever he played, his games were about disasters, and his
stories were about catastrophes. He told me innumerable times
about the sinking of the *Titanic*, sunk to the bottom of the sea
after colliding with an iceberg on its maiden voyage. In his story nobody survived except the captain, who died afterwards of
exposure and hunger, alone on an iceberg. I would like to speculate that his archetypal expectation of a soft breast full of warm
milk met at birth with the archetypal image of "iceberg-breast-
mother" and his death sentence. Another of his stories about
cold and death from exposure was that of Scott at the South Pole.

In his play with the little cars he enacted his fierce, sadistic,
oral, anal, and genital fantasies of the primal scene *(coniunctio)*.
He pushed the little cars one into the other, threw them against
the wall, and stamped on them with his big foot until they were
actually reduced to bits, claiming that he was "the Incredible
Hulk" (a green giant), an identification that made him feel like
Superman. At other times he was identified with the little cars
and the people in them, who were all killed. Sometimes he liked
to describe scenes from crashes where bodies had been smashed
up and dismembered, and he played at killing his grandparents,
his parents, his sister, and myself with savage ruthlessness and
sadism which exhibited some psychopatic trends. He felt he was
"really" killing them, as when he was thus absorbed in his play
the boundaries between pretending and reality did not seem to
exist for him. His playing had a hallucinatory quality about it,
and I sensed that he might suddenly turn around and attack

me as he attacked the toys. Indeed, he did brutally attack children at school and once shot a teacher in the ear with a toy gun, permanently damaging her hearing.

His war games were very relevant, showing up his inner conflicts and his destructiveness. It was as if the opponents — German and British — were bound to destroy each other, and annihilation of both sides and a massive catastrophe were the usual outcome of his games. A compromise could not be reached, or even imagined. Not even the victory of one of the two opponents could be foreseen. Like the captain of the *Titanic*, he would, in the end, find himself the only survivor. Then he began to play at killing himself and telling me how he would actually kill himself by throwing himself under a car. He would then go to heaven, where he would at last be at peace and could laugh about all the unhappiness he had caused, or that had been caused to him.

At times he would regress, lying for session after session sucking his thumb, shivering and feeling cold, curled up like a fetus, back into the primal self. During these periods I had to nurse him, cover him up with a blanket, and talk to him as I would to a tiny baby; as in the case of John (Chapter Six), it was the sound of my calm voice that he found comforting. Both his extreme aggression, linked to his fantasized omnipotence, and his massive regression, linked to his feelings of total helplessness, were very distressing for me to share, as both states had a dimension greater than life. Then he became obsessed by fires and brought matches to the session. One day he almost managed to get a fire out of control before I could take the matches away from him. At home, too, he liked to start fires, and this was extremely worrying. While all this was going on in his analysis, his parents found having to cope with him at home increasingly difficult. They both came to see me regularly, but I did not succeed in getting them to see a colleague in their own right. The father also started acting out, and scenes and quarrels between them at one point escalated into a dramatic fight, after which the father ran away during the night in a state of confusion, taking Jim with him in a mad car drive. This scared Jim, making him feel uncontained and worse. However, in the course of this distressing event, Jim managed to feel a lot of affection for his father and close to him. In fact, it was thanks to Jim not going to pieces on that particular occasion and talking to his father that enabled his father eventually to regain his mind, and so the mad outing ended well.

After this episode Jim was extremely concerned about his father, and a much better relationship began to develop between the two of them. One morning he took his father's penknife without permission and unfortunately broke it. This made him anxious and guilty. In the session the following day he expressed a wish to write to his father in order to make some sort of reparation. The letter contained apologies, and while writing it Jim expressed major anxieties about his father getting angry with him because of the broken penknife. I interpreted this as Jim feeling that he had damaged daddy, and he feared this would make daddy very angry—mad with anger. He feared that his father would destroy him.

Following this session, Jim talked to his father and convinced him that he should come to see me. The father's attitude toward me and toward therapy had considerably changed since the previous year. He sounded sad and unhappy but hopeful. He admitted that Jim had improved since coming to analysis and said that it did not matter how long it had to go on as long as it could help him. He had difficulty leaving the room but was relaxed as he walked out. I felt that a solid working alliance between us had been created, which I did not feel existed between me and the mother, although she kept constantly in touch with me.

After his father's visit, Jim was filled with joy, excitement, and pride, wanting to make his parents, grandparents, and everybody happy. His feelings of happiness and love were uncontainable—as boundless and extreme as his feelings of hatred. His love and gratitude for me began to emerge, and thus, following Jim's achieving a better relationship with his father, we had some more positive sessions. I became his loved father in the transference, and we could reach a certain degree of integration while he experienced love and gratitude for me. This found expression in the story he dictated to me, imagining he was going to write a book. He had a grandiose fantasy of himself as a writer, which resulted in an almost immediate collapse in feeling threatened and bad and unable to become a writer or even to write. He became depressed. He spent several sessions trying to dictate the story to me. When he was pleased with my writing, his love and happiness were expressed by huge hugs, by jumping on my lap, pulling my hair and throwing himself into my arms in a way that had an excited, sexual quality about it. I interpreted his wish to get inside me and put some of his happiness into me so that I could share it with him.

He became frightened by the intensity of his feelings and ran away when such behavior began to take control of him. I said that he was afraid of wanting to do with me what he imagined mummy and daddy did when they were alone together. He called me "sex maniac" and ran away, attacking the wall immediately with a pair of scissors. I said that he was afraid of hurting me, which he was now doing to the wall with his penknife-willy.

As he had said that he had damaged his father's penknife, I added that his willy is a pen when it is a good willy and a knife when it is a bad one. "I wish I could kill you," he said. "I think you do and you don't," I replied, "because part of you feels I am good because I have written your story for you." Whenever I made a statement of this sort he would firmly deny it, acting out his wish to kill me by verbal and physical attacks. But if I insisted with my interpretation, he would eventually admit that I was right. What he really enjoyed was to give me false clues, so that I would have to work hard and rely on my own counter-transference feelings.

The story Jim dictated ends with the sea journey in the North

Sea, full of icebergs. This seems to me a clear reference to his early fantasy of meeting with the iceberg-breast. The reference to the dramatic episode represented in the sinking of the *Titanic* stands for a catastrophic damage in Jim's self-ego axis. The story of Scott's journey is also his attempt to symbolize his analytic journey, with me as the "driver," toward the safe land, out of the icy-cold sea of the unconscious. But the story has no conclusion—nor did his analysis, which had to end prematurely.

While Jim's relationship with his father had improved as a result of their shared ordeal and their mutual understanding, his mother, imagining that the two of them were ganging up on her, and feeling left out, persecuted, and paranoid, began to panic. In fact, I had always thought that while the father was openly disturbed and had had psychiatric treatment and breakdowns, it was the mother who was the most disturbed member of the family because she could not get in touch with any of her unconscious feelings; her shadow was totally split off and unattainable to her. She began to suspect that I, too, was on their side. She became demanding of my attention and was often on the telephone, ringing me at all times of the day and night when she felt too anxious and murderous toward Jim and excluded from my relationship with him. She wanted to push him out of his session and get his session for herself. She did not succeed; neither did I succeed in arranging analysis for her with another analyst, because she wanted me and nobody else. Eventually she turned to her own mother, feeling rejected by me, and decided to move and live near her in the country. This led to the termination of Jim's analysis. The family moved out of London, and Jim was sent to a special community boarding school, where, unfortunately, he did badly and was eventually admitted to an adolescent psychiatric in-patients' unit.

All this took place at the end of Jim's second year of treatment—just at the stage, I felt, when he had definitely begun to show improvement, and when he might have been able to release himself from merging with the mother. Termination of his analysis proved to be a disaster, and he became very regressed. He came to his last sessions in a state of rage and, in a violent temper, accused me of being all sorts of monsters, as he showed in his pictures. He said that he hated me more than ever. He was desperate, he threatened to commit suicide, and he refused to come to his sessions. Once he ran away from school in order not to come to see me and, during this period, drew pictures of me in the style of a monster and as an object or part-object. Finally he began to cry in desperation, and during his last session he told me that he did not want to go away but that both I and his parents hated him and wished him out of the way, and that anyway he would kill himself and die. Then, suddenly becoming sad and hopeless, he added, "It is like building my car. I have started time and time again. I think that now I have all the pieces, but I cannot finish the job." This was an extremely sad and desperate statement.

Then his mood changed. He threw a few pieces of furniture around the room, just missed me, ran out, and never came back again.

I then realized that the analysis had sunk before the defensive system of the "Iceberg Mother," and, like Jim, I was left with a great deal of rage and frustration for his upset, and also because I knew he was right. He was beginning to get it together, and although I did not know how far I could go with him, nevertheless I was beginning to see some results from all the work we had done together.

Nevertheless, I knew we would never be able to finish, as I also knew that although his mother had promised that she would bring him back if he needed it, she was only too pleased to get him away, as his progress in analysis was beginning to shake her and to bring into the open her unconscious destructive envy of him and of the possibility that he might not carry on being the recipient of the unconscious projections of her own madness. She was unconsciously envious of me because I could perhaps help him where she felt she had failed, and this was intolerable. He had to remain the container of her darkest projection.

As far as Jim's father was concerned, he was too weak emotionally to be able to support Jim in his fight for his own psychological survival, because the mother's position was so hard and inflexible. This stirred up enormous rages in the father and tended to make him blow up in a destructive, murderous way. Although he wished to, he could not help Jim in any way. And this is, unfortunately and tragically, the sad story of the premature termination of Jim's analysis.

Discussion

Following Fordham's theoretical view, one might speculate that Jim's primal self, at the onset of the deintegrative processes, could not unfold in the normal way, nor could it reintegrate the deintegrates that come into existence and are produced by these early deintegrations. The deintegrates were experienced as non-self and were instantly attacked and destroyed by a self-immunizing defensive system (Fordham, 1976; Jung, 1976; Stein, 1967), which prevented both emotional development and symbolic life. Tustin (1981) writes:

> At first the sensuousness of the infant in the state of normal primary autism, and his relatively undifferentiated, global awareness, combined with the adaptability of the mother arising from her "material preoccupation" protect the newborn infant from "nonself" experiences. . . . The way in which the infant develops awareness of the 'not-self' is crucial to his sense of individual indentity. . . . the psychotic child has encountered "not-self" in a way which he experienced as traumatic because he had not developed the necessary neuro-mental integration to cope with the strain. . . . In ordinary situations the first auto-sensual construct and the actual mother are not differentiated, thus unbearable frustration is avoided.

As for my own experience of working with Jim, his clinical material shows that he experienced sensations and impulses as total and absolute. For instance, the sensation of cold was, for him, icy-cold; hot was burning fire; soft was extreme softness, and hard was stone-hard. Each of these sensations was so intense and extreme in itself that it excluded and precluded any linking with its opposite, implying, as Tustin states, the lack of a "sufficient level of neuro-mental integration to cope with the strain" (Tustin, 1986). And many analogies with alchemical symbolism as described by Jung were thrown up in the material.

Jim's violence was usually triggered off by the slightest conflict with the omnipotent fantasy that he ought to be able to do, or to obtain, whatever he wished, whenever he wished it. He could not sustain any gap or frustration. Bion (1970), discussing the structure of the explosive personality in "Attention and Interpretation," states, "The intensity of the patient's pain contributes to his fear of suffering pain. Frustration and pain are equated." Later he stresses the impossibility of communication without frustration, stating that communication has to do with separation and feelings of loss and is, therefore, the precursor of mental space. He also adds that representation of mental space can be too restrictive to the explosive kind of personality and a conceptualization of mental space in such a person — as space enclosed within boundaries — cannot take place, due to his intolerance of frustration. The concept of space defined by boundaries cannot be acquired by these patients because they cannot accept any distance from, or substitution of, the object. Their frustration is too great, and nothing else can do. What Bion is stressing here is the patient's need for a perfect, eternal fit.

When the object (breast-mother) moves away from the place where it used to be, such patients who cannot, for the reason stated above, have a thought or a memory of the object as *other* can experience the absence of the object as a concrete bad presence of a non-object—"no thing" instead of nothing. This "no thing" fills up the empty space and can be attacked and blown up, as it was in the case of Jim. I feel that the "no-thing" has characteristics of Fordham's not-self object. Bion (1970) says:

Therefore excessive intolerance is likely to obstruct awareness
of realisation. The "no-thing" with its corresponding realisation of some object not present will be liable to destruction,
whereas "hallucination" will be favoured for its immediacy.
Thought consequently is not seen as offering freedom for development, but is felt as a restriction. By contrast, "acting out"
is felt to yield a sense of freedom.

Jim's frustration was so unbearable that it had to be evacuated all the time, these evacuations, due to their energetic discharge, being equated by Jim with volcanic explosions.

The images of the volcano and the iceberg, symbols derived
from natural phenomena, depict both the nonhuman level of
experience and the importance of the human being at the mercy of the unleashed elements. Both images contain immense
power and energy: the fire of a volcano is perennial, and its outbursts are unpredictable. Even when dormant, an internal fire
can occasionally awaken and the volcano be reactivated. The
terrifying and powerful image of a mountain spitting fire and
magma evokes total impotence, and Jim told me that if the volcano erupted, he would wait for it to kill him.

The iceberg, on the other hand, is just as powerful and paralyz-
ing an image. It is a frozen mountain of water whose energy
is unattainable owing to its frozen state, and so solidly cold that
not even the power of the sun or the surrounding ocean can
melt it. Its origins are as ancient as those of the volcano and
date back to the Ice Age. The bulk of the iceberg is submerged,
and this presents a great hidden danger to all ships at sea—hence
the reference to the *Titanic*. An iceberg can never fully melt,
just as a volcano can never be considered extinguished. I have
interpreted these two natural images as visual representations
of an impossible *coniunctio*, a catastrophic primal scene or a fa-
tal nonfit—a primal scene that could not occur without the
parental opposites damaging or destroying each other. In fact,
if we take Jim's symbols of the volcano and the iceberg as representing opposites such as the mouth-nipple or the volcano-daddy

and the iceberg-mummy, the iceberg-breast and the volcano-penis could not be conceived together in a creative intercourse, although the fire of a volcano would be needed to melt an iceberg. Neither could the mouth-nipple fit occur for Jim from the start. When we look at them as representing two opposite states or sensations within himself, we can well understand how a reconciliation would be impossible until these archetypal images were transformed psychically into some more manageable form.

In the sessions we were at times able to have some good interchanges, but such good moments were short-lived and seemed doomed not to bear fruit. Although Jim appeared to introject my care and my interpretations, he seemed unable to assimilate them and make them bear fruit in a constructive way. They remained unintegrated. On my part in the countertransference, I had to deal with my own primitive layers of the psyche; the strain that working with Jim put on me was considerable, requiring me to remain sane, and for this I needed a great deal of support from my own analyst and from my supervisor.

REFERENCES

Bion, W. (1970). *Attention and Interpretation*. London: Tavistock.

Edwards, A. (1978). "Schreber's Delusional Transference—A Disorder of the Self." *Journal of Analytical Psychology*, 23, 3.

Fordham, M. (1976). *The Self and Autism*. L.A.P., Vol. 3. London: H. Karnac Books.

Freud, S. (1905). "Fragments of an Analysis of a Case of Hysteria." *Standard Edition*, Vol. 7.

Hubback, J. (1984). "Acting Out." *Journal of Analytical Psychology*, 29, 3.

Jung, C. G. (1958). "Appendix" to "Schizophrenia." *Coll. Wks.* 3.

Jung, C. G. (1955). *Mysterium Coniunctionis. Coll. Wks.* 14.

Proner, B. (1983). "Attacks on Analysis." *Journal of Analytical Psychology*, 28, 3.

Stein, L. (1967). "Introducing Not-self." *Journal of Analytical Psychology*, 12, 2.

Tustin, F. (1981). *Autistic States in Children*. London: Routledge & Kegan Paul.

CHAPTER 8

THE ABSENT PATIENT

In this chapter I will attempt to combine Jung's theory of the archetypes with observable evidence of archetypal activity both in infancy and later life. To do so I will draw on the observations of an infant named Paul, and on clinical material from the analysis of an adult patient, John, using developmental concepts in order to bridge the two cases. The point here is to illustrate the way in which different archetypal images, from a variety of archetypes, are constellated in patients according to their experiences, both internal and external, at different developmental stages.

When John referred himself to the clinic, he was in his late twenties; he was a teacher who worked with deprived children. He looked much younger than his age, and was of medium height, very skinny and wiry. His complexion was pale; his hair was brown, his eyes dark, melancholic, and expressive. His face looked haggard and thin.

The style of his clothes—which changed continuously— seemed to preoccupy him a great deal. It appeared to me a strange combination of mismatched bits, which, I felt, reflected his inner emotional state. He took a great interest in shoes, which he changed often and which had to do, he told me, with feeling masculine and tough—especially when he wore heavy boots, which he seemed to display like weapons.

He agreed with my suggestion to come four times a week, although initially he had hoped to be seen only twice weekly because he felt the only ones in need of looking after were the children in his care. He had difficulty acknowledging that he might have some needs too, for the children in the home were his only concern; he couldn't take any time away from them, and looked after them with total dedication, day and night.

His account of his life depicted an unhappy childhood both at home and at school, and throughout it all were scattered long descriptions of illness and solitary play. He had had a difficult start in life; he was the second of three children born to a young, inexperienced mother who herself had suffered from maternal deprivation, having being brought up in a children's home. John described her as a warm, temperamental woman who, not surprisingly, had enormous difficulties in bringing up her children but was now doing well in later life. During John's childhood she had suffered from physical illnesses, and states of severe depression alternating with violent outbursts of rage. She seemed to lack an internalized good mother; she idealized motherhood, could not acknowledge her hostility towards the baby for fear of damaging him, and appeared to have been inconsistent in her methods of child care. She never physically abused her children, though she sometimes struck them. Her violence was acted out in fights with her husband.

John's mother told him that he had given her trouble even before his birth, which enhanced not only his guilt but also his omnipotent fantasies about his own destructiveness. After a difficult breech delivery, John had to be separated from his mother for two weeks, as she had developed a serious post-partum complication. He was thus exposed at birth to a long separation from his mother, with great implications for his later life, as the two never seemed to be able to work out a good emotional fit; the shared fantasy of having damaged each other omnipotently tainted their relationship and made it unsuccessful.

He described his father as physically strong and tough, though emotionally weak and dominated by his wife. He too had suffered from nervous breakdowns and depressions. He was prone to fits of temper and used to hit John for no apparent reason. The parents quarrelled frequently and violently, which at the time scared John and made him feel unsafe at home. This in turn contributed to the formation of his heroic psychology—the hero killing the monster parent.

While John considered his own and most other parents bad, he felt that his own parenting of the abandoned children was very good, and he idealized his parental role. His siblings did not figure very much in the picture he drew of his childhood; his sister, four years older, and his brother, four years younger, were both introduced as blurred figures. He spoke of them without affection and with a mixture of jealousy and contempt.

At the age of seventeen he became involved with drugs. He eventually had trouble with the law; an elderly minister, however, took an interest in him and introduced him to working with disturbed children—which, he found, gave him a chance to feel better about himself. He was fairly pleased with his work, which he seemed to perform reasonably well, although he felt that his professional efficiency could be improved were his symptoms to improve.

In the social sphere, he complained of unsatisfactory relationships with both men and women, whom, it soon emerged, he both idealized and despised, complaining that he was unable to have any real fun in the social context as he could feel neither closed to nor relaxed with either women or men. While in relationship with women he doubted his sexual potency; with men, to whom he felt attracted, he feared his own homosexual wishes and was terrified of being thought of as gay.

Recently, however, after the breakdown of a love affair, he again

developed anxiety attacks, which incapacitated him and interfered with both his work and his private life. Through the years
he had also suffered from a variety of physical symptoms of a
psychosomatic kind—pains in his legs and stomach, headaches,
dizziness, eating difficulties, and a total inability to relax. He had
sought help for these from various doctors without any results,
and he began to feel that they might all be psychological, as his
own doctor had told him. During his panic attacks he used to
feel sure he would fade away and die.

At the start of analysis he was often breathless, very tense,
and he kept scanning me and the room through half-closed eyes.
In the session he was in an almost constant state of tension and
fear; he kept on talking, both to keep me at a distance and to
placate me, for he expected that as an analyst I would want him
to talk. Although his body revealed his tenseness and fear, he
related his past painful and disturbing experiences in a monotonous and unemotional tone.

I suggested that he lie on the couch, and he did so after overcoming considerable anxieties; he seemed to comply out of fear.
He kept his body stiff and looked uncomfortable and unrelaxed,
as if ready to spring up and run away.

From the account John gave me of his early life and childhood, he seemed unable to recall warm and happy moments
within the family or at school. The relationships within his family sounded very disturbed and arbited by archetypal patterns.
He mainly remembered his parents' constant and violent quarrels (bad primal scene fantasies), which confirmed his feelings
of great isolation, emptiness, and misery.

Following the first interviews, as a result of my countertransference I experienced opposite feelings: serious doubts about
his suitability for analysis, a sort of dislike for him (I almost rejected him), yet also a powerful wish to help him. I was struck
by his considerable vitality, moved by his needs, which I felt were
genuine, and impressed by the remarkable work he did with the
children in his care. The intensity of my countertransference

feelings proved to be a warning about the kind of difficulties we would encounter in the course of his analysis, the degree of his pathology, and the intensity of his transference to me. While writing this case up, I came across an interesting book about a child-care workshop held at the Tavistock clinic, *Psychotherapy With Severely Deprived Children,* edited by Mary Boston. It contains a paper by Shirley Hoxter, "Some Feelings Aroused in Working with Severely Deprived Children," which I found extremely relevant to John's analysis. Hoxter writes:

> The children discussed in this book showed that their lives were dominated by a continuing need to keep at bay the intolerable emotions of their past experiences of deprivation.... The crux of the child's deprivation may be perceived by the absence of one adult who, parent-like, shows constancy of care by being sufficiently present, and emotionally available to be receptive to the child's feelings and "think about them." (Hoxter, 1983)

To add a Jungian concept to this very clear statement, I would say that these children live in archetypal fantasy worlds, and unless the "thinking" is done by an adult who cares, they remain in the grip of the archetypes and their experiences of life do not become humanized. Emotions are extreme and impulses uncontainable. Good experiences are highly idealized, and bad ones unbearably bad. Hoxter continues:

> The staff of children's homes are especially vulnerable to being treated with contemptuous indifference. Like the therapists they are made to feel very fully what it is like to be ignored, despised, helpless or even unreal and nonexistent. Like the therapists they feel themselves to be regarded by the children as mere rubbish collectors... By helping the staff to bear having a clear look at the subtle complexities compounding their identification with the under-privileged, we can both help to deepen their awareness of the child's feelings and also to obtain a more self-respecting appreciation of their value.

I felt that this statement was doubly true in the case of John, as not only was he identified with the children in his care, but he carried inside a mother who had been brought up in a children's home. Thus his choice of work could be considered both an attempt to rescue his inner "abandoned baby" as well as his mother and her inner deprived baby.

As John's analyst, in the transference I had to endure being ignored, despised, omnipotently disposed of, and filled up with rubbish; all along I had to accept his massive projections and identifications, make sense of them, think about them, and while holding the situation in space and time, survive his merciless attacks on my existence, my feelings, and my own retaliatory murderous wishes towards him. Nevertheless his analysis broke down, after seventeen months of difficult work, as a result of his tremendous conflicts in returning to treatment after a break or a holiday.

John's case raised in my mind the question of technique and of the availability of the analyst towards a patient who misses so many sessions that one begins to wonder if he can be considered in analysis at all; in this case, verbal interpretations did not seem to affect the patient's analytic behavior. It was as if he had a compulsive need to act out a ruthless revenge against the parent/analyst by whom he felt abandoned, and which he was not able to do as a baby with his mother. Thus the analyst had to experience being the abandoned baby for a very long time, and to struggle with the pain and distress before any transformation in John could take place. I discussed my work with a senior colleague, and this enabled me to carry on the analysis and to explore the limits of the analytic attitude, as well as to extend my understanding of John's problems and my own capacity to withstand his acting out in the transference.

Theoretical Background

In terms of Jung's theories, when I first saw John he presented an overdetermined identification with a rigid persona, which he referred to as "the feeling of wearing a mask." This served to hide and disguise the most infantile, primitive, and undifferentiated part of himself—the shadow. Thus a dissociation had occurred in John's psyche.

When discussing this state of affairs, Jung wrote:

> Such dissociations come about because of various incompatibilities. For instance, a man's present state may have come into conflict with his childhood state...and has thus become unchildlike and artificial and lost its roots. This presents a favourable opportunity for a...vehement confrontation with a primary truth. (Jung, 1951)

Fordham developed this statement further in his paper, "The Importance of Analysing Childhood for the Assimilation of the Shadow." As he points out,

> How important is the shadow of maturity, i.e., infantilism, in arriving at a wholeness which is the aim of individuation. (Fordham, 1973)

Fordham goes on to say that

> The constant interaction between the maturing psychic organism and the environment is what produces development. If the infant's daily needs are not sufficiently met, we know maturation is retarded or stopped and false solutions are arrived at which later on cannot be used to meet the task of life demanded as an adult. (Fordham, 1973)

John's one-sided development and overdeterminedly flat and "masklike" defensive system (persona) had the function of hiding and disguising the chaotic, undifferentiated side (the shadow) that interfered with his daily life. That is, the most infantile and primitive parts of his personality (the infant within) had to be kept very much at bay for fear that they would take over and flood his adult self with all sorts of undesirable impulses and affects, such as the ones he experienced as a baby when, as Fordham says, his "infant needs were not sufficiently met."

Some observations made about a twelve-day-old baby, Paul, illustrate the sort of feelings I felt John had to struggle with and which I feared he might be overwhelmed by. The baby Paul is going through a state of total chaos and disintegration while being changed by his mother before a feed, from which he is left shaken, but recovers fairly soon. I quote from the case observations:

> As soon as he settled down to feed he was interrupted. The mother proceeded to dress him, and as soon as the new nappy was placed under his bottom he began to cry again. He went red in the face, rubbing his hands over his eyes frantically. His left hand got caught in his Babygro and he cried angrily. The mother remained calm and managed to get his hand through the sleeve quickly. He was crying now quite steadily, having got into some sort of rhythm of taking a deep breath and crying out loudly, taking another deep breath and screaming it out again. He did not seem to hear his mother talking to him. He looked absorbed in getting rid of his bad feelings—the frustrations of being pulled about and being made to wait had all become persecuting. Comfort was not available to him at this moment. The mother buttoned his Babygro, picked him up, and put him over her left shoulder, and he stopped crying.
>
> She started feeding him, and the feeding was proceeding well when, ten minutes later, the doorbell rang and the midwife arrived with a student to examine the mother, which meant that Paul's feed had to be interrupted. The interruption lasted four minutes. He was in the cot no longer than five minutes, but it may have seemed something like an eternity to him. He began to cry, escalating into screaming, which drowned all conversation. It sounded like a protest and rage that could go on forever.
>
> As soon as the midwife had gone, the mother picked up Paul and began to walk about, talking to him and hoping to soothe him. He had soaked and dirtied himself in his fit of desperate and explosive rage. Paul slowly changed his tone of crying. He was crying more softly, and although the mother was holding and talking to him, he did not seem to hear her voice. He began to scream again while she tried to change

him, and he would not be comforted or calmed while this went on. She was concerned and upset, and said she had never heard him cry like this before. She held him close to herself after having changed him, soothing and comforting him, rocking him gently and telling him, "What a naughty mum you have." Finally he calmed down, but now and again he gave out a deep sob. His lower lip quivered and his mother offered him the breast. He seemed too worked up to feed.

The sequence of deintegration-reintegration followed by a short spell of disintegration, when the baby appears fully absorbed in expulsive activities-inability to take in the milk, breathing difficulties, screaming expulsion of feces, urine and tears — suggests that the infant is in a state of total persecution, frustration, and rage, although nothing too dramatic has happened to him according to our adult point of view. It seems to me, however, that this is a manifestation of a baby in the grip of a "bad breast" archetypal experience, which only the comforting holding and caring of the real mother can, in the long run, relieve. Let us imagine that due to the mother's prolonged absence, or her not being in touch with the baby's needs, the disintegrated state of the infant cannot be met, and he is left unheld for too long in such a crisis; for the baby the situation becomes unmanageable, and in order to survive he needs to adopt some very primitive defenses, called "defences of the self" by Fordham, which are activated for the purpose of survival.

The absence of the mother in flesh and blood, or her failure to meet his needs, leaves the baby at the mercy of the negative pole of the mother archetype, which can be experienced as a malignant, cruel, murderous attack against him by the "horrible witch."

The archetypal image of the "horrible witch" often appeared in John's materials. At times I "was" the witch for him in the transference, but more often so in his dreams. Witches came out of old tombs, ancient doorways, dark passages; beautiful girls suddenly turned into horrid crones, and the only thing he could do was to hide in order to save his life.

At the beginning of his analysis and during breaks from it, John dreamed a great deal. His dreams were rich, archetypal Jungian dreams with vivid, often terrifying images. He once said that both in reality and in dreams he so suffered from such terrors that he felt the only place for him was "sitting on a fence between the two "worlds." Hiding away and sitting "on the fence"—being neither "in" nor "out," but on the border between the reality and fantasy—described very well, I think, the borderline defence system that John adopted in order to save his life in the very early stages of his childhood. These defences had of course become obsolete and unadapted to his adult personality and the expanding needs of his ego. However, John could not alter them because changing the system and lowering his defences would have been experienced by the baby inside him as having to meet the dangers of a confrontation with the witch, and thus being killed. He also experienced, in his dreams, his child self as gone away to the moon in a rocket, or as becoming a small dot and fading away. To me all these seem possible ways of "not being" there and of not being caught by the "murderous witch."

While this was going on, in the transference I experienced John as in a state of constant terror and always on the verge of jumping up from the couch and running away. He kept me at a distance, pushing himself as far as possible away from me physically, scanning me constantly with his eyes and trying to nail me down. His talk tended to veer away from interpretations of the material in the transference into his own rationalizations and ready-made interpretations related to reality (defensive use of reality)—which, I felt, tended to fill me with rubbish and were aimed at confusing me. He constantly reversed to a concrete level.

Most of the time, John seemed to chew my interpretations in the room and spit them out as soon as he ran away from the session, or to swallow them whole without biting into them and then ask for more. Thus he tended to get what he called "psychological indigestion," and I was experienced as the feeding "bad mother" who caused this. In the session he seldom seemed to inhabit his body or his psychic space, and this, I felt, was in order to prevent me from getting inside him. Nor did he attempt to get inside me; rather, he adhered to me and tried to get under my skin, which in turn was as far as he allowed my interpretations to penetrate him.

A paper by Esther Bick, "The Experience of the Skin in Early Object Relations," defines very well the situation I am trying to describe:

> The skin of the baby and of its primal objects in relation to the most primitive binding together of parts of the personality not as yet differentiated from parts of the body... can be most readily studied in psychoanalysis in relation to problems of dependence and separation in the transference. The thesis is that in its most primitive form the parts of the personality are felt to have no binding force amongst themselves and must therefore be held together in a way that is experienced by them passively, by the skin functioning as a boundary. But this internal function of containing the parts of the self is dependent initially on the function. Later, identification with this function of the object supersedes the unintegrated state and gives rise to the fantasy of internal and external spaces. (Bick, 1968)

The function of the skin as described by Bick—containing the parts of the baby self—would, according to Fordham's theory, be performed by the primal self in an integrated state. What Bick calls the parts of the baby's self would correspond to deintegrates of the primal self, which in order to reintegrate need to be met with the holding fuction of the mother's ego. Failing this, they cannot be satisfactorily reintegrated, and either remain split off or tend to be reincorporated, undigested, in a superficial way. When the deintegrates remain unintegrated and/or split off, they lend themselves to all sorts of archetypal imagery and tend to be experienced by patients in visual forms, disembodied and two-dimensional.

I am not going to dwell here on John's view of his father or on his experience of me as the father in the transference. However, his relationship with his father was certainly archetypal, primitive and violent, corresponding both to his infantile fantasy and to the collective, undifferentiated disturbed psychological and emotional level of his own internalized father. As neither mother nor father could become "human" in John's eyes and experience, he kept experiencing them unconsciously in the form of archetypal monsters or gods.

In recent years Kenneth Lambert has contributed to dealing with the problem of emerging consciousness in various papers, a recent one of which appears as a chapter in his book, *Analysis, Repair and Individuation*. He writes:

> At the oral stage, the inability of the mother to meet the infant's feeding needs and his need to be held, etc. may foster an agonising sense of emptiness and despair. At its worst, apart from the infant's death, his libido may move into the service of what Fordham has called 'defences of the self'. In this situation there is maximal awareness of emptiness and danger, but minimal consciousness. The personality and helpfulness of another person are felt as overwhelmingly threatening, dangerous, destructive, so that, despite the sense of weakness and emptiness of one's own personality, all efforts of a helping person are warded off as if in a fight for existence... upon observations of transference phenomena on the part of certain patients suffering from damage incurred in early infancy, they have formulated the theory that in them a heroic or do-it-yourself psychology develops. It issues into notions of (1) a 'grandiose self' which obscures all feelings of emptiness and weakness, and of (2) 'idealised good parents' projected onto others and the analyst, who are nevertheless always found in the end to be either useless or poisonous. In this situation we find the condition of maximum alert awareness with minimal consciousness and maximal delusion. (Lambert, 1981)

When describing the emerging of consciousness, Jung states that the "first manifestation of the child is as a rule a total unconscious phenomenon":

> The initial stage of personal infantilism presents the picture
> of an "abandoned" or "misunderstood" and unjustly treated
> child with overweening pretensions... The epiphany of the
> hero (the second identification) shows itself in a correspond-
> ing inflation... Once the reef of the second identification has
> been successfully circumnavigated, conscious processes can
> be cleanly separated from the unconscious, and the latter ob-
> served objectively. (Jung, 1951)

The Child Archetype

The material that John brought to me at the start of his analysis featured both the themes of the "abandoned child" and the
"emotionally battered infant." The children he looked after, and
the "battered infant" whose needs had not been sufficiently met,
often appeared in his early dreams in the image of a real infant
or of a baby animal left out and abandoned in the cold at night,
and which he rescued and looked after. In his life the "mythical
dangers," as Jung calls them, were causing him to live through
an agony of panic, fears and terrors of all kinds, mainly to do
with his body letting him down, as in the situation where there
is "maximal awareness of emptiness or danger, but minimal consciousness," as Lambert puts it.

In John's analysis this state of affairs was very intense during
weekends and breaks, but also at the beginning and end of each
individual session. The space "in between" John and me in the
session never seemed right; it was either too close or too distant. When too close, it was experienced by John as an attack
on his physical and emotional integrity, which scared him as
much as his feeling of isolation and emptiness. His level of anxiety and terror was highly apparent, and he seemed to rush into
each session in an attempt to bypass his total resistance to it.
He arrived, dashed into the room and rushed onto the couch,
and he disappeared in no time at all as soon as the session was
over, having struggled with the need to stop. When I commented on this, he said it felt as if I left the country after each ses-

sion, and he was afraid I would never come back. His sense of
continuity of himself and of time and space was very shaky. For
John, as for a baby, nonverbal communications were the most
important. I had to be very much in tune with him to pick up
all the slightest signals coming from his body in terms of postures,
expressions, and so on, and to make sense of them; and I noticed that my presence was more important to him, as was my
facial expression, than what I actually said. I also observed that
at times the tone of my voice and the degree of light in the room,
the temperature, and all kinds of minute details and sensations
could have a dramatic effect upon him during the session.

Along with his fear and anxiety that I would disappear, and
in an attempt to defend himself from it, he displayed a need
for a pseudo-independence and a panicky anxiety at allowing
me too close to himself emotionally—as if he risked being gob-
bled up by me (the devouring mother/breast), or that he might
devour me (the baby's fantasies of devouring the breast).

At the genital level, too, he was afraid of not being able to
control his sexual urges so that he might act out his genital wishes
in a violent way. The fear of being sucked in by me, or sucking
me dry, alternated with a wish to merge with me, which in turn
generated (a) anxieties of annihilation, and (b) fear of the castrating father, given his secret genital wishes towards me, the
mother. Usually, manic flight occurred at this point in the session, in reality or out of analysis altogether. I interpreted that
he was experiencing, in the transference, the deprivation of his
early infancy, and my leaving him—at the end of each session,
or during breaks—was equivalent to the mother's abandonment
of his infant self. This evoked such unconscious frustration, distress, and panic that he became terrified and had to control his
anxiety by cutting off and splitting. He was, in the transference,
experiencing the stage of development in which he had very
little perception of himself and the mother as separate beings,
but rather as an undifferentiated whole. His projective identification was massive; he expected me to retaliate as the baby

would expect the breast to retaliate, and hungrily eat him up.

In the first six months of his analysis his attendance record was perfect, and he could have been considered the ideal patient. He seemed to be taking in my interpretations, appeared to be insightful, and produced many dreams that seemed to point to great activity in the unconscious. I was highly idealized and felt by him to be the perfect analyst. He was, as he put it later, being a good child, the perfect child who had to behave well for fear of being rejected — the good child he had in the past experienced his mother as wishing him to be, and he complied in order to please her. This situation changed dramatically after my first long holiday, which he experienced as a catastrophic abandonment, with me as the totally bad mother who attempted to murder him. From this moment his acting-out as a rejection of me began, and escalated with all sorts of testing out, behaviors and difficulties which proved hard for both him and me.

I think that the good child's behavior was a compliant superficial adaptive defense dating back to John's latency, around the time of his younger brother's birth, when his mother "dropped" him to completely dedicate herself to the baby, and the father was not around. John remembered having to get to primary school all by himself. The bad rejecting behavior that brought out the "bad child" in him could be like what he felt he had to enact at the age of four to five, but which he had to suppress when he realized that his mother could not cope with it. In turn, the theme of having been abandoned by his mother and by me evoked, in the transference, his very early experience of abandonment and separation from his own mother.

The "bad child" did not want to come to the sessions and often ran away from them, as the children John looked after ran away from the children's home. In one dream just before my holiday, he was watching an educational television program about teaching youngsters how to die. In his words:

> I watched the screen, which showed a woman hanging paral-
> lel to the screen from a very thin string knotted around her
> waist. Then somebody cut the string. I was terrified; I felt the
> woman was going to fall and hit the ground, but she did a
> quick somersault and fell onto a cushion that appears to have
> been underneath. I was puzzled and could not make any sense
> of it. What has it got to do with dying?, I asked myself. I
> thought, I cannot understand it. If she lands on a cushion how
> can she die?

John seemed to be struggling with his wishes to control me while
denying the feeling that my going away, the cutting of the string
by which he felt attached to me, felt like dying, or killing me.
The rationalization was a defence he often used to protect himself from affects, and to reason himself and me out of "any
danger."

He related the dream to me as if it were "a story watched on
a television screen." It seemed to be happening outside himself,
and he was watching it but not in it. Thus he managed to split
off its affective contents, keeping them in the screen because
he dreaded fantasies becoming real, as inside and outside, fantasy and reality, were little differentiated to him, and his boundaries appeared to be very blurred. Opposing feelings of
helplessness and omnipotence created constant conflict in John's
life and analysis; thus his omnipotent control and denial used
to come about in order to avoid experiencing my departure at
the end of each session—he "smuggled [my] image out, like a
photograph to hang on [his] wall." Or he imagined "putting [me]
in [his] pocket" and taking me with him wherever he went. "Taking me inside" might have been too dangerous, because his baby
moods might have instantly turned me from totally "good" to
totally "bad," deadly dangerous to have inside. He could thus only
allow himself to smuggle me out as a two-dimensional photograph in his pocket or a flat picture upon his wall. Having me
in his pocket gave him feelings that he could magically control
my comings and goings, making me appear and disappear, very
much like a baby feels he is magically controlling the movement

of the mother/breast. I felt that all this was in order to blot out the unbearable realization of my absence, which he unconsciously dreaded and which the infant side of him equated with the catastrophic experience of early life. The feeling of frustration arising from this realization—that attempts to control me did not succeed—brought about a total ruthlessness, setting up an equally powerful need for revenge. He could not have me, so I would not have him. He began to miss sessions. One could say that he identified with the "absent breast" and became the "absent patient." I had to be both the baby who survived, waiting, and the mother who did not fail him.

At first the sessions missed were the ones after breaks, which I interpreted as him angrily wanting to pay me back. The he missed sessions before breaks; I interpreted this as him wanting to pay me back in advance. Then he began to feel that, having missed a lot of sessions, he could not come back for fear of my retaliation. He was afraid of my angry attack on him, like his mother's nagging when he failed to comply with the behaviors she expected of him. He rejected my interpretations of his anger with me for having deserted him, and he denied any anger and jealousy. His absence was justified by a defensive use of reality. He could not come, he was too busy. The interpretations did not produce any changes in his behavior, although he slowly began to understand, at the intellectual level, that the unconscious roots of the problem lay in his interactions with his mother in early childhood and infancy. Yet he could not see that missing sessions was his way of attacking me, or that I could be concerned in any way or upset by him. My feelings and objective reality could easily be impounded by him. He always had plenty of impeccable and "real" reasons why he could not come.

He began to stay away from analysis for longer and longer stretches of time, suddenly returning to see if I were still there. I kept interpreting his analytic behavior, his defences, his anxieties, but his attendance record did not improve. I felt that the only thing I could do was to hold the situation in space and time,

and remain alive and together, thus resisting his destructive murderous attacks, like the mother who held Paul through his stormy
crisis. It is interesting to note that John paid for all the sessions
he missed, and when I pointed out how he was wasting his money as well as attacking his analysis and attempting to kill me off,
he admitted that he wished to exasperate me so that I would
end up rejecting him as well as terminating the analysis. His delusional system prevented him from realizing how I had been available and he had rejected me. I felt he was pushing me to the
limit, wanting me to confess that I was a parent/analyst who
could not cope — like his mother, who could not handle him
when he was a child. He also told me that his not coming to
sessions when he felt very angry with me was a way of avoiding
actually attacking me physically, which he both wished and did
not wish to do.

Thus I came to realize that his missing sessions had several
meanings. They could be understood as retaliatory — that is, making me suffer by missing him in the same way that he missed
me when I left him. They could also, as we have seen, be a way
of protecting me from a fantasied outburst of physical violence
derived from his frustrated libidinal wishes, both oral infantile
and genital adult, as he could not actually possess my body and
soul. He would try to arouse my jealousy by telling me about
his love affairs with various girlfriends, all of whom seemed to
want him and whom he used or rejected as sex objects.

I feel, however, that the main reason he tried to stay away from
analysis as much as he could, hoping that I would kick him out,
was his fear of regression into an addictive dependency from
which he dreaded never being able to recover. In brief, it seemed
that his weak ego feared being engulfed in the psychotic contents of his unconscious; he dreaded a psychotic breakdown. His
struggles for independence seem to me to stem from the situation described by Lambert above (see p. 148).

In the second year of his treatment, during the fifteenth
month of analysis, John came back very distraught one day, af-

ter a long absence, telling me that his paternal grandmother had died and that he had spent some days at home with his parents; he felt his presence was much appreciated by his father, who had been very depressed by the loss of his mother. John was not fond of his grandmother, to whom he often referred as "the old witch," but coming face to face with her death had shaken him, and his father's grief had touched him deeply, making him think for the first time that one of these days he would lose his parents too. All these feelings, coupled with the genuine affection and gratitude his father had shown him for being there and supporting him, made John cry a lot in the session, and some deep feelings were stirred up in him. A few days later he brought a dream in which, with my help, he managed to kill a witch who lived in the basement of a building where I used to "run a nursery class," with him as my assistant. He killed the witch with a knife and chopped her up; he then burnt her and threw her ashes in the nearby river—because, he told me while reporting the dream, this is the ritual way of getting rid of the witch "forever."

John linked the dream to the death of the grandmother, and also to an as yet vague realization that he did not want either me or his parents to die because he was beginning to become aware of his feelings, his real love for me and for them. However, this remained one solution—and, the dream aside, a magical solution. When he came to sessions after that, he brought many reports on his daily life and the way in which, over recent months, it had begun to work for his good. His work was going well. He had been promoted to a very responsible position, his relationships with friends and colleagues seemed satisfactory to him, and his financial situation was flourishing—so much so that, notwithstanding my having had to increase my fees quite considerably, he had been able to put aside money over the last two years and was now buying a house. His ability to relate to the children and to their distress seemed much improved.

His physical symptoms had almost disappeared. He could have

fun in life now, and at times even feel relaxed. For these reasons he said that although he was sorry to stop, he was thinking of leaving analysis. Considering how he had actually attended it, I commented that I thought these results seemed rather magical to me, that a full analysis had not taken place, and that the core of his personality remained unchanged. However, I agreed to stop the following month—but warned him that he should in no way consider himself out of danger of falling back into the same old problems again. At the same time, to agree to end the sessions seemed to me the only sensible thing to do, at least for the time being.

During the two last sessions he told me that he had decided to marry a girl he had been going out with for the previous nine months and whom he had known for eight years. When I commented that he had decided it all by himself and left me out of it completely, he admitted he was afraid that I might disagree and spoil his feelings by some clever interpretation. Obviously the "witch" was still there; I pointed this out to him and suggested that stopping the treatment might be the way of killing her. However, when we parted he was able to express some genuine feelings of gratitude mixed with angry frustration for having had to compromise rather than destroy and get rid of me, as he had initially wished to do, or to have me exclusively to himself.

A few weeks after our last session I received an invitation to his wedding. He was marrying someone related to psychotherapy. This could well be a coincidence, but knowing him I would also think it had to do with his inability to symbolize his experiences, as he tended to live out his fantasies in a concrete way. He seemed to be telling me that he could not have me as an analyst forever, so he was going to marry into an "analytic family."

I sent my best wishes for his wedding and left it at that. About nine months later he contacted me again, saying that he had thought a lot about our work, had missed it, and decided he wanted to come back into analysis again. I offered to see him again and discuss what it was all about. I had to tell him, however, that if he decided he really wanted to return to analysis I might have to refer him to a colleague, as I was unable to see him. He looked most disappointed and shocked, as if it had never occurred to him that I might not be there whenever he needed me. As I interpreted this to him, he agreed that he was most upset by what I had told him. However, he still felt he wanted to come see me. He then began to tell me that the reason he wanted to return to analysis was that his wife was soon going to give birth, and this both scared him and angered him — he felt he did not want a baby at that time. He then told me that his wife was against his having analysis at this stage because the birth of the baby would be a costly event, and they had no money to spare for John's needs. I felt that he had come to me as to a lover, to compensate for the loss of attention from his wife that the birth would entail, and that this was the reason he did not want a child — unconsciously, he experienced it as a rival sibling. I interpreted all this to him and linked it up with his early sibling rivalry, his father's love affairs during the time mother was at home looking after the babies, as well as to the long period during his analysis in which he had left me, the mother/analyst, alone, looking after his baby-self, while he missed sessions to go out with all sorts of lovers. Now it was his wife's turn to be cheated and abandoned with the baby, as he had agreed with her that he would not go into analysis. I suggested that if he really felt he should commit himself to analysis this time, he should speak to his wife first and then we would see what could be done.

He made a further appointment, but he never came back, nor did he let me know what he intended to do. He owed me for the last few sessions and did so for over a year, in spite of my sending bills and the occasional reminder (he eventually paid).

I am not clear as to the extent to which John had been able to integrate his unconscious contents. The only major shift that did occur during the time we were working together was, I felt, his stepping off the fence upon which he had perched his whole life, and his choosing to go down into the outer world of "reality," moving further way from his grandiose and terrifying archetypal imagery—which as a result began to fade into the background, John closing the door to the depths of the unconscious psyche, the underworld that disturbed him with all its monsters and horrors. At the same time, what he managed to integrate of his shadow allowed him to become much more creative, both in his work and in his personal relationships. Thus we can say that our work together made him more adapted to reality and distanced him from the immediate danger of a psychotic breakdown, and that it also made him aware that in case of need he may still be helped by analytical psychotherapy. It had also allowed him to achieve a degree of separation from the parent/analyst, which he had not been able to achieve, during adolescence, from his real parents. The technique used in John's analysis was very often much like the one applied in working with adolescents, as he seemed to have remained stuck at this stage of his emotional development.

In the beginning of the analytic interchange, John fought against his awareness of me as a person in my own right because it meant I was separate from him, and this felt unbelievably painful to his infant self. I experienced John as an unsupporting, demanding, moody, and erratic partner, or as a very controlling baby, often totally unaware and unconcerned of my needs or of me as a person, treating me mostly as an object of both love and hate. A great deal of reductive-adaptive analysis was necessary to reduce some of his grandiose fantasies. His ego strengthened, and he became capable of avoiding being inflated by archetypal imagery, precipitating a psychotic breakdown to which his attacks on the analysis were connected; but he also managed to integrate a more adult ego capacity, which enabled him to move out of his predominantly adolescent state.

REFERENCES

Bick, E. (1968). "The Experience of the Skin in Early Object Relations." In *International Journal of Psychoanalysis*, 49, 4.

Fordham, M. (1973). "The Importance of Analysing Childhood for the Assimilation of the Shadow." In *Analytical Psychology: A Modern Science*. L.A.P. London: H. Karnac Books.

Hoxter, S. (1983). "Some Feelings Aroused in Working With Severely Deprived Children." In Mary Boston, Ed., *Psychotherapy With Severely Deprived Children*. London: Routledge & Kegan Paul.

Jung, C.G. (1951). "The Psychology of the Child Archetype." *Coll. Wks.*, 9, 2.

Lambert, K. (1981). *Analysis, Repair and Individuation*. L.A.P. London: H. Karnac Books.

CHAPTER 9

SEPARATION IN ADOLESCENCE

In this final chapter I will focus on how the deintegrative-reintegrative processes of the self unfold in adolescence, and how these influence the ego at that particular stage of its development. Jung, and Jungians in general, have in the past focused mainly on adolescent states of mind as observed in adult patients who, as Jung saw it, were in the grips of the "child" archetype, with its positive, creative "forward goals" or implications of negative "stuckness" (Jung, 1940). Marie-Louise von Franz has also described such patients (von Franz, 1982), the easily recognizable adult patient who is afraid of growing old and who tends to identify with youthful heroes and their deeds in search of everlasting youth. We must, therefore, distinguish between adolescence proper and adolescence as a state of mind, which we can define as archetypal in nature.

With regard to adolescence proper, Jung wrote that "conscious differentiation from the parents normally takes place in adolescence with the eruption of sexuality" (Jung, 1930). In his paper, "The Theory of Psychoanalysis," Jung wrote—in response to Freud's views on infantile sexuality—that although a relatively

161

...early budding of eroticism exists in the child early on....This element gains in strength as the years go on, so that the Oedipus complex soon assumes its classical form. The conflict takes on a more masculine and therefore more typical form in a son, whereas a daughter develops a specific liking for the father, with a correspondingly jealous attitude towards the mother. We would call this the Electra complex. As everyone knows Electra took vengeance on her mother Clytemnestra for murdering her husband Agamemnon and thus robbing her— Electra—of her beloved father.

Both these fantasy complexes become more prominent with increasing maturity, and reach a new stage only in the post-pubertal period, when the problem arises of detachment from the parents. This stage is characterized by...the symbol of sacrifice. The more sexuality develops, the more it drives the individual away from his family and forces him to achieve family independence. (Jung, 1913)

"The problem of detachment from the parents," as Jung puts it, is renewed and recapitulated in all experiences of separation from birth onwards. In the inner world, unconscious archetypal motifs will therefore be constellated at each phase of development, which will reflect the various stages in the resolution of past conflicts, compounded by anxieties and conflicts related to the new stage.

In Fordham's *Children as Individuals* we find an important— and still highly relevant today—statement about adolescence:

The roots of the adolescent's uncontrollable turbulence lie in infancy, when his mother and later other members of his family comprised his "society"; it was in relation to them that the prototype of later patterns of behavior were laid down.

In all early periods, maturational processes pressed him away from prepersonal ruthless drives towards forming a perception of himself and his mother as a person about whom he has felt concern; now at adolescence the prepersonal structures revive in response to the less personal role he is expected to fulfil. So the infantile roots are needed if he has to find his identity in a new pattern of living. Omnipotent phantasies result in attacks on parents and on society that stem from the manic defences of infancy, the sources of heroes and heroines. Depressive episodes, depersonalising, hysterical acting out and splitting of the ego are not at all infrequent and often constitute a kind of "normal insanity." The ruthlessness characteristic of these states is proverbial and when they predominate an adolescent needs support and a kind of indirect holding such as the mother provides for her infant in crises, rather than the direct control of discipline which only provokes more rebellion.

An adolescent comes into direct contact with the culture pattern and the collective unconscious. (Fordham, 1969)

In other words, with the upsurge of sexuality the young person has to undergo a major deintegration in order to be able to integrate all the major changes which are occurring both in his body and in his or her new experience of life. This deintegration will reactivate those archetypal motifs in the unconscious related to the difficult task of acquiring adult sexual and intellectual capacities, compounded with the urge to live these out—moving away from home and severing childhood ties to the parents. It is a stage of renegotiating one's life-style and identity, and brings about conflicts and powerful emotional and anxiety states. Unconscious fantasies and primitive collective archetypal motifs become activated, and a regression-progression dichotomy sets in, usually acted out in relation to parents, teachers and society.

Shifts from excited to depressed states, from impotence to omnipotence, from insecurity to arrogance, from extreme passivity to frantic activity, and so on, occur frequently, often to extreme degrees; the novelty of the experience constellates the archetypes of the hero and heroine, and we all know how much hero worship is a feature of adolescence, from football players to pop singers, actors and politicians. The adolescent "fan" tends to create his own heroes, identification with whom seems to serve to provide supportive models of people who have already and successfully accomplished the task the adolescent is to accomplish himself. These idealized hero-figures are those the young person can model himself upon and draw strength from — as opposed to the parents, the devalued heroes of the past, who must lose their idealized role in order to be left behind by the adolescent, together with his childhood dependency upon them and their authority.

The parallel to the hero motif is the motif of sacrifice, which will be constellated because it relates to all initiation rituals. For instance, primitive archetypal motifs related to the hero motif — images of death, mighty struggles, abandonment and loss — surface in dreams and fantasy, creating conflicts and distress in the adolescent. Such conflicts may activate, at the unconscious level, archetypal images of the death of the child and the murder of the parents. The aim of such images is to bring to consciousness and allow a working through of the ending of childhood as a stage of life. At times this experience can bring about extreme despair, and the adolescent, taking it concretely and becoming overwhelmed by distress, may put an end to his or her own life. In such cases the symbolic metaphorical level is not attained, and instead of the symbolic birth of the hero/heroine, which would promote a step forward, what takes place is death, the sacrifice of the young person's life. Suicide is in fact one of the greatest causes of death in adolescence, whether consciously or unconsciously motivated — accidents, drug overdoses, and so on. In turn the unconscious, in working through infantile dependency, may bring to consciousness images of the parents' death, and this again is likely to overwhelm with guilt the adolescent who interprets them concretely; it may even push the very disturbed to act out and commit a crime. This tends to happen because, as Fordham states in the above passage, "the prepersonal structures revive in response to the less personal role the adolescent is expected to play. So the infantile roots are needed if he has to find his identity in new patterns of living." Infantile roots entail a regression to a pre-symbolic, undifferentiated mode of experiencing, which pertains to infancy and is therefore archetypal.

The "murder of the parents"—which means, in infantile language, getting rid of the parents in rage by usurping their power—is a motif which belongs to the unconscious fantasies of the pre-Oedipal and Oedipal stage of development, and which becomes regressively activated again in adolescence, in the thrust to acquire full genital potency. The unconscious fantasy of the murder of the parents may be disguised, as for instance when an adolescent says that he (or she) cannot leave home or do whatever he wants for fear that his parents will be broken-hearted or may not be able to survive the adolescent's moving away—hence he must sacrifice himself in order to protect and save the parents. Confusion arises here, because the adolescent is projecting regressed parts of himself onto the parents, as well as disowning his/her murderousness and wish to be free of parental dependence, which is felt to be "bad"; the adolescent is identifying with the "good" wish to look after and protect the parents as a way of dealing with the unconscious guilt generated by the "bad" wish.

Another common confusion is that between the real parents and the parental imagos:

> In reality the whole drama takes place in the individual's own psyche, where the "parents" are not the parents at all but only their imagos: they are representations which have arisen from the conjunction of parental peculiarities with the individual predisposition of the child. The imagos are activated and varied in every possible manner by an energy which likewise pertains to the individual; it derives from the sphere of instinct and expresses itself as instinctuality. (Jung 1912)

Parallel with the motif of the death of the parental couple is that of the death of the child, which is generated by regressive tendencies and which brings to the fore early infantile fantasies of starvation, abandonment and helplessness. Directly deriving from them are anxieties, consciously manifested by the adolescent, of not being able to "make it," fears of not finding a job and not being able to earn one's daily bread. These anxieties in normal situations provide positive action in the adolescent, when he manages to positively identify with the caring adult in himself; in pathological situations, however, his anxieties may paralyze him and induce extreme passive and negative self-destructive behaviors of all kinds. Jung states clearly that

> The road of regression leads back to childhood and finally, in a manner of speaking, into the mother's body....Whoever gives up the struggle to adapt and regresses into the bosom of the family, which in the last resort is the mother's bosom, expects not only to be warmed and loved, but also to be fed. If the regression has an infantile character, it aims — without of course admitting it — at incest and nourishment. (Jung, 1912)

Hence the more the adolescent is stuck in a regressive state, the more he will use such defensive mechanisms as denial, manic triumph and omnipotent grandiose fantasies in an attempt to manage guilt and shame, and to overcome ego failure.

Thus far I have tried to describe how the change of life — that is, adolescence — is experienced in the inner world at a fantasy level, and the kind of drama that needs to be enacted in the psyche so that the young person can move to the next stage of life. As I have pointed out, it is the archetypal contents of the psychic drama which blur the line between reality and unconscious fantasy. Owing to the deintegrative processes, the ego is in great turmoil, weakened by attempting to withstand the pressure from the unconscious; it breaks down and often disintegrates. This is why we often witness an adolescent confusion in which the inner drama is acted out in reality.

In fantasy the death of the child and of the old parents will eventually give rise to the birth of "new" ones — the new youth and the new couple who can only be born out of the ashes of the old ones.

I hope it will be clear by now that the bodily pole of the archetype, experienced in the body and monitoring the instinctual drives and bodily changes, goes hand in hand with spiritual change — the instinctual and physical experiences acquire a metaphorical mental representation. Thus the transformative processes inherent in deintegration and reintegration can reach a new and more adapted level, and life can go on. However, the achievement of adult genital identity is the major developmental task and an extremely difficult one to perform smoothly. As we have seen, a regressive tendency in the unconscious can easily set in and reverse this life task, with the aim of keeping the adolescent in the grip of extreme anxiety, stuck between the parents and unable to move on, either externally or internally.

This regressive tendency is often reinforced by concurrent anxiety in the parents caused by the obviously worrisome behavior of the conflicted youth; but it is also due to the parents' own identification with the adolescent-or the reactivation of unresolved adolescent conflicts in themselves — that they may try to control their children by means of projection, adopting a clinging or rejecting mode of behavior in relation to the distressed or disturbed child. Letting go requires sacrifice on both sides, and in the process a great deal of pain is experienced by both parents and children alike, analogous to the pain of actual physical birth — a new and major change is taking place in the family. A major deintegration will also take place in the mother and father, who will have to accomodate themselves to the changed family situation and prepare themselves to enter the second half of life.

Managing this situation takes time, and entails risks on both sides, the acceptance of limitations and responsibilities — inherent to the new situation — by both parties, as well as acceptance of the advantages and disadvantages the change may bring about. It is here that Jung's emphasis on the fantasy of sacrifice appears to be pertinent. In his paper on the etiology of neurosis he writes:

> The unconscious fantasy of sacrifice, occurring some time after puberty, is a direct outcome of the infantile complexes....
> The fantasy of sacrifice means the giving up of infantile

wishes. I have shown this in my book [*Symbols of Transforma-*
tion] and at the same time have pointed out the parallels in the history of religion. (Jung, 1913)

In *Symbols of Transformation*, Jung writes

> The natural course of life demands that the young person
> should sacrifice his childhood and his childish dependence
> on the physical parents, lest he remain caught body and soul
> in the bonds of unconscious incest. This regressive tendency
> has been consistently opposed from the most primitive times
> by the great psychotherapeutic systems which we know as the
> religions. They seek to create an autonomous consciousness
> by weaning mankind away from the sleep of childhood. The
> sun breaks from the mists of the horizon and climbs to un-
> dimmed brightness at the meridian. Once this goal is reached,
> it sinks down again towards night. (Jung, 1912)

The Absent Father and the Crucifixion of the Hero-Heroine

The following is the dream of a seventeen-year-old boy; it is
drawn from the second year of his biweekly therapy:

> My mother is in bed. She looks like she is crying. I go close
> to her to comfort her. Suddenly I scream with pain, my back!
> My father's huge penis has violently penetrated my anus,
> pierced my belly and penetrated my mother's vagina, and there
> I am, terrified and in agony, nailed as if crucified between them
> in their intercourse.

The dreamer, Larry, was uneasy about reporting the dream and
still very shattered by its contents. His associations highlighted
his own behavior, putting himself in that situation in order to
comfort the mother—who, he felt, was upset because his father
had ill-treated her. The image of crucifixion aptly summarized
the position in which the boy was stuck, and the reason why
he had been transferred to me.

Larry's clinging to his mother and his coming in between the
parents was still happening in reality; it developed in the transference as well. Before meeting him I had received a telephone

call from a male colleague who told me that I would be soon contacted by a woman about her her son who needed help, but that I should not tell the boy who had referred him to me because my colleague knew the boy's father, who would never have forgiven him for the referral; the father always pretended that there was nothing wrong with the boy except that he was lazy and a good-for-nothing. The whole business thus had a conspiratorial flavor. Then the mother called me to complain mainly about Larry's laziness and massive failure at school. I suggested that, given his age, the boy might call me so that I could assess whether he felt he had a problem and whether he wanted help with it. The mother seemed to feel that this was not necessary, that I was being difficult and that I should take her word for it. I then had to explain that I could only treat Larry provided he wanted me to help him; eventually she accepted my view, though not without some astonishment. Larry eventually called me, and we agreed that he should come to see me and that we would take it from there.

Larry arrived at the appointed time accompanied by his mother, a verbal, determined, sophisticated and emotionally cold businesslike woman behind whom, I felt, Larry tended to hide himself. He was an attractive boy with a wiry body; in contrast to his mother, he was rather scruffily dressed in jeans and running shoes. He seemed to wish to impress me with an "I couldn't care less" attitude. His mother began telling me about his failures at school, which she identified as the problem; she spoke of all that she and her husband had tried to do to help him, and how they had failed. Short of tying him down to his desk with his schoolwork in front of him, she had tried everything (including spending a small fortune on private tutorials); but he kept on failing, and she had come to the conclusion that she had better try psychotherapy, which neither she nor her husband thought especially convincing in its results. She had been told, however, that it helped with difficulties at school.

My first impression of Larry was that he was a bright and

talented young man who by failing was attacking his own mental capacities, hence crucifying and castrating himself while projecting the cause for this onto his father and society at large. His behavior tended to provoke persecutory superego interventions from his father and other authority figures. I had to stop the mother in order to ask Larry for his version of the story, but he really seemed at al loss as to what was going on; I felt he looked rather humiliated by his mother's report. I pointed this out to him, adding that it must not feel good for him to be publicly humiliated, and that I did not believe that he didn't care. At the beginning of the interview he sat on the double settee next to his mother, like a little boy holding on to mummy's skirt. He appeared to relax and began to look around, and at length when his mother left the room and I proceeded to interview him on his own, he moved from the settee to an armchair opposite me. I found this move interesting and suggestive of his own interest in therapy, something from which a therapeutic alliance between the two of us might develop.

Adopting his mother's manner of reporting, he carried on enumerating, almost proudly, all his scholatic failures: he was three years behind in his schoolwork, and had behaved so badly in the classroom that he had now been expelled from the school. "They," he said, meaning the headmistress and the teachers, "were a bunch of pigs," so it did not really matter, and anyway his classmates were a boring lot because they were all babies three years younger than he was. He told me that his real interests lay in photography and political revolution. School was really boring, and his parents and the teachers just had to resign themselves to the fact that it was not for him. His father had given up on him long ago, and Larry did not think he was academically inclined like his sister—who also was boring, who only talked of architecture and was a show-off anyway.

I commented that I could not see why he had to be a failure at school if he could be good at politics and photography, but we could find out about this if he came to see me. To this he replied, "I think I will come, but do not think I am coming because I want to go back to school." I said that I was not a teacher or a parent, and that my only interest was in finding out, with his help, what was going on inside him which was preventing him from succeeding at school, since in my view being good at school was nothing very extraordinary.

He looked bemused but agreed to see me, and throughout the two and a half years he was under treatment he kept an impeccable attendance record. In the sessions he soon became very controlling and possessive of me. In the room he nailed me to the chair with his constant stare, which I experienced as controlling and always trying to show me up. If I was not constantly on the ball he would pick at me and contradict me, demanding my total attention. It felt like he was a demanding baby, wanting his mother's eyes constantly focused on him. He played about with the time, arriving late and not wanting to leave when the hour was up. He always had something extremely important to tell me at the last minute, which seemed to require extra time, and when I pointed out to him that he was manipulating the time by arriving late and wanting to leave late, he became very angry and gave me a tirade on political lines. We soon came to talk about his revolutionary stance. Did I know how keen a revolutionary he was? He had been caught by the police, during a riot, throwing molotov cocktails with another youth—well, he was only throwing stones, but I should not mess about with him. This was the message I picked up, and I interpreted it as his wanting to scare me and put me in my place. He said that his family had a tradition of rebels and patriots and brave people who were not afraid to fight tyrants. His Spanish paternal grandfather was a hero and had committed suicide in jail, having been arrested by the dictator's police and preferring to kill himself rather than give away his comrades' names. He was a hero and had been an anarchist who died for his beliefs in the cause of freedom from oppressors. "Like myself and the sort of people who tell you what to do," I added. "You could say so," he answered, giving me a fierce look while tensing up as if ready to strike me.

I felt I had touched upon a sore area, so I commented that it must have been very sad for his own father to have lost his daddy in that way. A child would surely have mixed feelings about a father who is a hero, but who at the same time abandons him in order to die for some incomprehensible reason. Besides, if he was a just man why was he in prison? My comment made Larry thoughtful, and then he told me the very painful story of how his heroic grandfather had killed himself, swallowing the crushed glass of his own spectacles. "He died a horrible death," said Larry proudly, his eyes full of tears, "but he did not speak." To avenge him, his sister became a partisan and she too bravely supported the cause of the oppressed. They are mentioned in history books. Larry's father was a baby at the time and never really knew the grandfather, but he suffered because the grandmother became depressed and he had to look after her. She wanted Larry's father close to her at all times, and so did all the old aunts.

It appeared that the pain and distress about his grandfather's death had been locked up inside Larry and his family for all those years, and they could only allow themselves to feel proud of his bravery. The thought of the violent death he suffered was too painful; it also made for a glorification of suicide. Indeed, Larry was unconsciously suicidal and very definitely at risk when he entered therapy.

After this session, Larry allowed me to speculate with him about what the child in his father, as well as the child in himself, felt about the "absent father," both his dead grandfather and his own father, who until then had been conspicuously absent from the sessional reports. Larry told me that his father was an important man and seldom at home. He was a famous lawyer and university lecturer, was always busy and had lots of students and political friends to entertain him. When he was at home he went into his study, where he read hundreds of books and listened to classical music, and he could not tolerate any noise in the house. Larry hated reading books and loved pop music. His father had often rebuked him for making noise. He had never played with him, as far as Larry could remember. He would talk for hours on intellectual matters, both with Larry's mother and his sister. He despised Larry's ignorance and his left-wing political views; he himself was rather a liberal. They had nothing in common; even when Larry had shown his photographs to his father, who admired them — they really were beautiful — he had not placed much importance on them. He told Larry that instead of wasting his time with that hobby he ought to apply himself to schoolwork and other more worthwhile activities.

While Larry was talking about his father, I perceived in his voice and bodily posture a mixture of envy, admiration, rage and despair. I put this into words for him, saying that he felt his father had no faith in him, and that this prevented him from having any confidence in himself and his intellectual potential and capacities. He was deeply affected by this interpretation; he denied it vehemently, saying that he did not care, that he did not have any respect for his father's political views, that his father was a coward and an egotistical man, a dictator. All this came out with a mixture of spite, hatred, rage, and an emotional vehemence that prompted me to say that he seemed too worked up about the issue not to care, as he had asserted. This turned him against me, and he threatened to walk out if I did not stop such talk immediately.

I had now become the hated father in the transference. Larry stopped talking to me, pulled his legs and arms closer to his chest, and gave me a defiant, murderous look of such intensity that I experienced, there and then, something like a blow on the head. Larry kept silent, looking at a point on the wall a few inches above my head. His expression changed as if he had seen something frightening. He said there was a crack in the wall above my head. After a while he began talking again and mentioned that somebody he had seen while on his way to me today had been hit on the head. It was a man and there had been a nasty fight. He had felt quite upset, he told me. Now I was able to link up his murderous look, my sensation of having been knocked on the head, his violent anger and hatred for his father's intellect, the fact that I had become his hated, clever father in the transference, and that he had wanted to murder me. It was my thinking capacity, which he experienced as cold and penetratingly persecutory, that had caused his emotional upheaval. He had felt cornered by me in the session, much like he felt cornered in the presence of his "superior" father. Yet I told him that by attacking my head and his father's mind, he was also attacking his own mind, and this is why he kept feeling inferior.

Following this session, a great deal of material surfaced about the relationship between his parents, and how he perceived his father exploiting his mother and yet being stuck to her and dependent upon her all the time. For as long as he could remember, his mother had always had to accompany his father wherever he was going, leaving Larry and his sister at home with nannies because of his father's social engagements. His father's professional success counted more than anything else, while he himself, Larry thought, did not count at all. Fortunately his nanny was really lovely and loved him; in fact she was wonderful to him. Then, when Larry was about five, his mother dismissed her because she had become jealous. Apparently the nanny was beautiful and his father had noticed her, so Larry lost her; from then on he was looked after by servants he did not like. I commented that the picture he conveyed to me was of his father successfully taking his mother away from him at a time when he really needed her, and that his mother had colluded with his father in abandoning him. However, this message was also complicated by the other stories he had told me about his father ill-treating his mother and making her cry. In the transference Larry was extremely curious about my other patients. He asked about my husband and, through ingenious questioning, found out about my whole family. It was quite clear that he could not tolerate me having other relationships. He occasionally came out with snippets of information about my life; I felt I was being closely observed and spied upon. He even admitted driving around my block at night with friends, on purpose, to check if I was in and asleep; he tried to figure out, by which lights he could see, which room I slept in.

All this material allowed us to work on his jealousy and rivalry with both father and sister for possession of the mother, his constant feeling of being the loser, and his wish to be as potent as his father: not only to be admired and loved and looked after by both his mother and sister, but also by the world at large — and of course by me, who he constantly complained was not really interested in him. He also complained of not having any real friends, at least not as many as his father and sister had, because they were both successful and admired. Worst of all he didn't have a girlfriend, which he found especially humiliating. All this material culminated in the dream I reported when introducing the case of Larry, towards the end of the second year of his therapy.

This dream allowed Larry to see to what extent he was clinging to his mother, thus placing himself, emotionally, between his parents, who he feared would forget all about him, happily engaged in intercourse, were he to leave them to themselves. In fact, in the countertransference he would at very odd times suddenly come to my mind in between sessions, distracting me from the relationships I was engaged in, and therefore managing to recreate in the analytical relationship something akin to his intrafamilial relationships. This enabled me to understand what Larry's father was undoubtedly feeling — anger and resentment of Larry's intrusion into his relationship with his wife.

So the dream reported above highlighted, in a striking and synthetic way, all the themes on which we had been working, and which Larry was thus eventually able to integrate. In the process he began to move away from his mother and became once more interested in learning. He successfully made up the years he had lost at school and progressed with his education.

In order to obtain a positive feeling for his father, he devised an ingenious scheme. He asked his father if he could use his office for doing his homework, because at home he had too many distractions and temptations, such as the television and his stereo. His father agreed, which meant that after Larry had finished his homework the two could spend some time together and so become closer. His attitude towards his father changed quite dramatically. Now he was the "good" one, and the two would have liked to put all the blame and resentment for their past conflicts onto the mother: the two men were going through the previously-unthinkable process of ganging up against "the mother," myself included. Although this shift created some problems in the analysis, such as acting out and missing sessions, Larry eventually came to understand his homosexual love for his father, as well as his own wish, in the past and present, to set the parents against each other in order to win their love. I interpreted that this must have started when he was small, the baby in the family, and that it was quite unnecessarily still going on, causing him all the pain we had observed, and the impossibility of letting go of his childhood bonds.

I will stop this case study here, with the happy ending of Larry's reconciliation with both his external and his internal father, and point out that it allowed him to recover his lost self-confidence as well as his brilliant intellectual capacity. He continued his studies and went on to study film and to become a director. Thus he found his own way of succeeding and pleasing his parents, whom he could now love as well as hate when he became angry with them. He did not need to sacrifice himself any longer; his therapy had set him free.

The following case study also involves the motif of self-sacrifice—in this instance, the patient's feeling that she had to sacrifice herself in order to protect her unstable and unhappy mother from the repercussions of a failed marriage.

Beth was seventeen years old at the time of her referral. I saw her once a week over the last nine months of her last year at

secondary school. She had asked her mother, who was in therapy, to find out about possible treatment for her, as she felt things
at school were worrying her. She was an oustandingly brilliant
student, praised and supported by her teachers and the students
because she was willing to help her friends when they were experiencing difficulties.

Everybody considered her a perfect girl. She was a child from
a mixed common-law marriage between an Anglo-Saxon Cath-
olic and a Moslem father. She had a lovely face, a light brown
complexion, long black hair, and deep oriental eyes. Although
considerably overweight, she moved elegantly and with poise.
She spoke in a soft calm voice which could become shrill and
extremely piercing when she was under the pressure of emotion. Her body, however, conveyed to me the impression of primitive fear. She giggled when embarassed and tended to withdraw
if she felt I was being too direct, as if scared of my potential
insight.

Her father was the most distressing element in her life. She
was the only daughter of her parents' common-law marriage, but,
being a Moslem, her father had another wife and family in his
own country, to which he would periodically return, often for
years at a time, until he came back full of guilt and of affection
for Beth and her mother. Everything went well until the next
time he departed, when Beth's mother had a breakdown. The
mother had had a difficult childhood, including the loss of her
own mother when she was a child. She was very unstable and
infantile in her emotional reactions. She could tolerate neither
her husband's long absences nor his double life, but neither could
she leave him. She began drinking and attempted suicide, which
resulted in the return of her husband.

This actual life situation, and the inability of the parents to
decide whether to separate or to continue living together, caused
Beth a great deal of pain, and their violent and passionate fights
in her presence had so scared her as a child that it was now impossible for her to express any murderous, violent feelings what-

soever. She had become the parent of the infantile parts of her
mother's and her father's personalities, with the result that she
felt there was nobody who could take care of her own infantile
needs and distresses. Her self-containing capacity and her identification with the holding mother was locking her child self in
desperate isolation. She demanded too much from herself, and
in this she was supported by her outstanding intellectual abilities, and by her incredible capacity for work. Until her final school
year she had managed to keep the distressed and scorned baby
inside her, tucked in and out of reach; but with her "A" level
examinations impending, her anxiety made her defensive system crack, and some difficult feelings had begun to leak through
from the unconscious. This, of course, had been fostered by the
deintegrative process related to adolescence, which she was trying
to fight with all her strength for fear of becoming like her mother,
which to Beth meant becoming emotionally incontinent.

In the transference it soon emerged that she had to please
and impress me all the time, and I could not reach her baby part,
which she kept projecting onto her parents. It felt as if I could
only provide a place for her where she could unload some of
her complaints about her mother and father, and so receive a
little bit of sympathetic understanding. As the therapy proceeded
and she became convinced that I knew what a good girl she was,
a less perfect girl began to emerge. She began to mess about
with the times of her sessions, forgetting to come and then suddenly turning up at the wrong time and getting upset if I would
not see her. She was behaving like her father, returning home
unexpectedly, and I was supposed to behave like her mother,
who allowed him back on his own terms. The fact that I would
not allow her to see me except at her appointed times made
her angry, and she would not accept it. For a while she stopped
seeing me, the excuse being that she was too busy with her examinations. I wrote her a note saying that we ought to discuss
whether she should terminate analysis, and left it at that. Her
mother became anxious about Beth's not seeing me, and tried

to intervene. I supported the girl's decision, saying that she had the right to decide for herself but that I would like to discuss the issue with her and not with her mother. This made the mother feel rejected by me, and she went to the director of the clinic where I worked and angrily accused me of not taking her daughter's situation to heart. Eventually Beth returned to me just after her eighteenth birthday, and as her father was due to return.

In the session she talked about her fear that her parents would begin fighting again — arguments in which she hated having to take sides. For instance, her father had written to her saying he would not return if she did not also want him back, as he could not promise to stay with them forever. She said she felt differently from her mother; she would be genuinely happy to see him return, and she wished only that he could take her with him to visit her stepbrothers and stepsister in his own country. She said her father was afraid that she was on her mother's side, but she wanted to tell him that she was not. She loved them both, but hated taking sides with them. She also felt she was being used as a judge by both parents, and so she wanted to be left alone and free of them; but she also worried in case they killed each other during one of their violent fights, were she not there to stop them. I commented that in not coming to see me, she wanted to test out my reactions as to whether I could tolerate letting her go, or whether I would get in an emotional state like her mother, or violently angry like her father.

At the next session she was much more subdued. She told me immediately that her father was arriving earlier than expected. She had been unable to sleep for excitement and fear. She looked confused and was tearful, and tensed up as she spoke. I asked for what reason she was so scared. Her mother's safety, she answered, and burst out crying.

It slowly emerged that her father had in the past beaten his wife, and on one occasion had even followed her round the flat brandishing a cleaver, possessed by jealousy and threatening to kill her. The fear and helplessness Beth had then experienced still paralyzed her now, and while she was recalling this she went white in the face and began to feel sick. I said that she was now reexperiencing the awful fear of the past, and this was why she had felt so bad about the news of her father's return. Beth was surprised that a distant memory could still be so powerful. She paused, and then said that her father with the cleaver in his hands was a terrifying image. In Beth's case this image of the archetypal "bad father" had been experienced in reality; it was therefore understandable that she could not let go of her violent feeling. The violent reality had prevented her from experiencing in fantasy her wish to kill the parents when she felt persecuted by them, and only now could she begin to let go of her fear and her pain.

However, in reality the father's visit went well. Beth was able to talk to him, and together they made plans for her move to the university, which her father was very proud of and warmly supported. She wanted to become a doctor and applied for a place in a medical school outside London, taking advantage of her father's help. In the meantime the parents decided to sort out their relationship; at last the father returned again to his own country, from where he kept in close contact with Beth. The mother was helped by her therapy, and was eventually able to let go and come to terms with the breakup of her marriage. Beth now began to talk about her impending examinations, and spent many sessions discussing her own worries in relation to the present situation, her school friends, her weekend job, and finally a boy who seemed to find her attractive. She had begun to move from the violent "primal scene," and was now able to concentrate on her own worries, those appropriate to her age. She had found support from a male teacher at school who was good to her and praised her a great deal.

When it was time for her examinations, she appeared sad to leave the school and her friends, particularly her teacher. I related this to myself and the approaching termination of her therapy, and she was able to admit that the work we had done together had helped her. She did well in her examinations and was accepted by one of the best medical schools in the country. Before leaving, Beth came to say goodbye. She looked quite different. She was an attractive young lady now, slimmer, well dressed, and much more aware of her femininity and her looks. She told me she had a boyfriend, and while the problems with her mother were still present in reality, she now dealt with them differently. She could now leave her mother as she no longer felt responsible for her survival. She had to get on with her own life.

Both cases above involve adolescents who remained stuck in an infantile relationship with their parents, and were unable to proceed further because of a negative father complex which became constellated in their unconscious as a consequence of the father's absence from or lack of interest in them when they were small children. In both cases, the absence of the real father helped produce the image of the bad, terrifying father which paralyzed both analysands, keeping them attached to the mother, whom they both felt they had to protect from the violent attacks of the murderous father. During the course of both analyses, some of the patient's own anger and violence in relation to the parents was worked through in the transference-countertransference, and this constellated the image of the good father-analyst. This subsequently allowed Larry and Beth to free themselves from the grip of the negative primal scene fantasies in which they had been locked, and in this way they were both able, after much hard work, to move on in their own right, as independent members of the adult world.

REFERENCES

Fordham, M. (1969). *Children as Individuals*. London: Hodder & Stoughton.

Franz, Marie-Louise von (1982). *Puer Aeternus: The Adult's Struggle With the Paradise of Childhood*. Boston: Sigo Press

Jung, C.G. (1912). *Symbols of Transformation. Coll. Wks.* 5.

Jung, C.G. (1913). "The Theory of Psychoanalysis." *Coll. Wks.* 4.

Jung, C.G. (1930). "The Stages of Life." *Coll. Wks.* 8.

Jung, C.G. (1951) "The Psychology of the Child Archetype." *Coll. Wks.* 9, 1.

CONCLUSION

Over the course of this book I have attempted to give an account of my analytic work over the years, with both children and adult patients; I have also attempted to illustrate clinical and theoretical issues related to analytical psychology as practiced in the developmentalist "London school" of Michael Fordham and his followers, which lays particular emphasis on the "inner child" and its manifestation in the transference-countertransference. Fordham founded the London school in the late nineteen-forties, his interest in children having stemmed from his own training and from his experience with young evacuees during the London Blitz.

In the fifties, Michael Fordham made a great contribution to the field of Jungian child psychology by applying Jung's theories of the self, of the archetypes, and of individuation to both childhood and infancy. In effect, to apply the theory of archetypes to infancy is to assert that the child is predisposed towards developing archaic ideas, feelings, and fantasies *without* their being implanted in him and *without* him introjecting them. Fordham postulated that the infant's instinctual discharges are modified and modulated by the experience of being mothered, and by the infant's discovery of background environmental images which both fit and evoke his experiences. In this way the developmental approach comes to meet archetypal theory, rooting archetypal images in the "red" end of the archetypal spectrum, i.e. at the bodily pole of the archetype.

It is at this level—in the realm of instinctuality—that one can speak of archetypal experiences brought about, in the infant, by his primitive instinctual discharges. Without the holding provided by the mother, both physical and emotional (the maternal reverie), these would remain raw and unintegrated. The mother helps the baby to make sense of the world and of himself, and to transform and modulate the archetypes in a manageable form. In the same way, the holding provided by the analyst — both interpretive and beyond, in the transference — and his/her maternal reverie (which is, according to Fordham, an "emphatic, concordant countertransference") provides the patient with a transformative experience of solid and safe boundaries within which a satisfactory reintegration can take place.

In the first chapter, where I discuss the unfolding of the self in infancy, I draw upon both infant observation and material from the analysis of an adult patient to show how ego growth cannot come into being without an experience of oneness, and how the basic conflicts of union and separation are indispensable to self-realization. Coming apart and getting together again with the mother enables the baby to build up an internal and external sense of space and time, which in turn allows the processes of separation and individuation to begin taking place.

Most of the patients discussed over the course of the book seem to have had to endure an experience of premature, traumatic, and distressing separation from the mother in early infancy, either because of the mother's or the baby's hospitalization, or because of maternal breakdown and/or depression, or because of other adverse circumstances. To varying degrees, in each case these factors seem to have interfered with the baby's healthy psychological development. In the case of Mary, for instance (see Chapter Three), an unconscious negative mother-baby relationship developed into a magic archetypal world of witches, nasty baby princesses, and ugly monkeys. Because the relationship with the mother affects all other relationships, the constellation of the "bad mother" archetype will cause the child to experience an equally "bad" relationship with the father; in other words, it will contaminate the other relationship as well. Thus a "bad" primal scene fantasy, with all its negative implications, will in turn be constellated in the child's unconscious.

In Robert's case, the mother's depression and his premature birth gave rise to extreme separation anxieties, violent jealousy, and sibling rivalry, which all told crippled his very gifted nature. Thus one can say that infants who have experienced repeated, premature, and lengthy separations from the mother at the onset of life are prone to develop negative unconscious fantasies of parental objects. This is due to their precocious experience of unbelievable levels of frustration, rage, and distress in the absence of maternal holding; the norm is for babies to begin separating from and relating to the other *when they are ready for it*. I have thus come to believe that the concept of frustration and tolerance to it is the starting point for archetypal images of "goodness" and "badness" in the psyche. This is the "archaic way of thinking" to which Jung refers and which he traces in myths and fairytales — thus our Chapter Four introduces the myth of Cain and Abel, a universal form of the drama of jealousy and sibling rivalry, which is compared with analogous events drawn from infant observations, where the same powerful emotions are fully expressed by one small infant and one toddler. While too much separation from the mother at the beginning of life endangers life itself, this becomes a necessity as the child matures. At the same time, the acquisition of a more realistic perception of himself and his abilities in relation to those of his mother prompts in the small child feelings of inadequacy, guilt, shame, and envy for the powerful forces of the mother and father, which the child fears he will never be able to acquire. The sensitivity of the parents to such anxiety and fear in their child enables them to facilitate the child's task of integrating his inadequacies without his feeling compelled to disown them. For instance, in his own mind Richard (see Chapter Five) attributed the departure of his mother to his having failed and disappointed her because of his bad behavior. He punished himself mercilessly and induced others to punish him because of his feelings of inadequacy and shame. These feelings surfaced in analysis and were worked through in the transference-countertransference. The boy was subsequently able to regain his self-esteem, as well as a good relationship with his own mother and the outer world.

There are, however, cases of a dysfunction of the primal self which is noticeable from the start. The integrating processes don't seem to occur in rhythmic sequences. The case of Jim (see Chapter Seven) illustrates one such unusual psychic situation, and underscores its endogenous origins. One would have to speculate that at the onset of the deintegrative process Jim's primal self could not unfold in a normal way, nor could it reintegrate the deintegrates that these events produced. The deintegrates were experienced as "non-self" and were instantly expelled and destroyed by the psychic self-immunizing defensive system which Stein (1967) and Fordham (1974) term "defences of the self."

Because of their intolerance of frustration, patients such as Jim cannot conceive of symbolic representations or conceptualizations of mental space. These patients cannot acquire a concept of space defined by boundaries, since they cannot accept any distance from or substitution of the object (Bion). Jim's frustration was so unbearable that it had to be evacuated all the time; he equated these evacuations—due to their energetic discharge—with volcanic explosions. The images of the volcano and the iceberg depict both the non-human level of the experience and the impotence of the human being at the mercy of the unleashed elements. These two extremely powerful images represent an unconscious primal scene fantasy of a very destructive kind; in coming together, a volcano and an iceberg would be mutually obliterated.

While Jim couldn't manage to integrate his powerful opposites, John (see Chapter Eight) could just barely manage to repair his damaged ego by identifying with the absent parent and turning me into the abandoned child. This defense mechanism typically appears in adolescence, when the conflict of separation from the parents becomes intensified. As Fordham posits, at this stage of life a young person reexperiences the turbulence of the infantile roots of the separation/individuation conflict; it is for this reason that, in working with adolescents, the transference-countertransference becomes even more pivotal as an analytic technique — i.e., a combination of flexibility and firmness within well-defined boundaries, which the patient tears down and the analyst sets up again, time and time again over the course of treatment, in order to help the patient establish his own identity and personal boundaries.

In the last chapter, and after examining the role parents play in facilitating or preventing the young person's detachment from them, I introduce the cases of a young man and a young woman, both of whom had remained stuck in an infantile relationship with the parents. Neither of the two could proceed further, the function of a negative father complex which had become constellated in the unconscious as a consequence of the father's absence from them, or lack of interest in them, when they were small children. In the absence of the real father, the image of the "bad, terrifying" father had paralyzed them, keeping them attached to the mother, a figure whom both felt they had to protect against the violent attacks of the murderous father. During the course of the analyses, some of their own violence and anger relative to their parents was worked through in the transference-countertransference, and this constellated the image of the good father-analyst, which consequently freed them from the grips of the negative primal scene fantasies in which they had been locked. In this way, both young people were able to move on in their own right.

I hope, given this multiplicity of clinical illustrations, to have managed to convey to the reader a picture of the unfolding of the self—in various patients at various ages (infant, child, adult)—as a process starting in infancy and continuing throughout life.

BIBLIOGRAPHY

Barnett, C. (1970.) "Neo-natal Separation: The Maternal Side of Interactional Deprivation." In *Pediatrics*, 46: 197-205.

Bick, E. (1968). "The Experience of the Skin in Early Object Relations." In *International Journal of Psychoanalysis*, 49, 4.

Bion, W. (1970). *Attention and Interpretation*. London: Tavistock.

————. (1962). *Learning From Experience*. New York: Basic Books.

————. (1962). "The Psychoanalytic Study of Thinking." In The *International Journal of Psychoanalysis*, 43: 306-310.

Bowlby, J. (1973). *Separation, Anxiety and Anger*. New York: Basic Books.

Brazelton, B. (1983). *Infants and Mothers*. New York: Delta.

Condon and Sanders (1977). *Studies in Mother-Infant Interaction*. New York: Schaffer.

Davidson, D. (1979). "Playing and the Growth of the Imagination." In *The Journal of Analytical Psychology*, 24, 1.

Edwards, A. (1978). "Schreber's Delusional Transference—A Disorder of the Self." *The Journal of Analytical Psychology*, 23, 3.

Fordham, M. (1969). *Children as Individuals*. London: Hodder & Stoughton.

————. (1985). *Exploration Into the Self*. L.A.P., Vol.7. London: H. Karnac Books.

————. (1978). *Jungian Psychotherapy: A Study in Analytical Psychotherapy*. Chichester: John Wiley.

————. (1982). "Some Thoughts on De-integration." (Unpublished).

————. (1973). "The Importance of Analysing Childhood for the Assimilation of the Shadow." In *Analytical Psychology: A Modern Science*. L.A.P. London: H. Karnac Books.

————. (1976). *The Self and Autism*. L.A.P., Vol. 3. London: H. Karnac Books.

Franz, Marie-Louise von, (1982). *Puer Aeternus: The Adult's Struggle With the Paradise of Childhood*. Boston: Sigo Press.

Freud, S. (1905). "Fragments of an Analysis of a Case of Hysteria." *Standard Edition*, Vol. 7.

Grotstein, J. (1985). "A Proposed Revision for the Psychoanalytic Concept of Death Instincts." *Yearbook of Psychoanalysis and Psychotherapy*, Vol.1, pp. 229-326. New Jersey: Concept Press.

Hoxter, S. (1983). "Some Feelings Aroused in Working With Severely Deprived Children." In Mary Boston, Ed., *Psychotherapy With Severely Deprived Children*. London: Routledge & Kegan Paul.

Hubback, J. (1984). "Acting Out." *The Journal of Analytical Psychology*, 29, 3.

Hultberg, P. (1988). "Shame: A Hidden Emotion." *The Journal of Analytical Psychology*, 33, 2.

Jung, C.G. (1926). "Analytical Psychology and Education." *Coll. Wks.* 17.

————. (1958). "Appendix" to "Schizophrenia." *Coll. Wks.* 3.

————. (1939). *The Archetypes and the Collective Unconscious. Coll. Wks.* 9, 1.

————. (1939). "Conscious, Unconscious, and Individuation." *Coll. Wks.* 9, 1.

————. (1955). *Mysterium Coniunctionis. Coll. Wks.* 14.

————. (1910). "Psychic Conflicts in a Child." *Coll. Wks.* 17.

————. (1939). "Psychological Aspects of the Mother Archetype." *Coll. Wks.* 9, 1.

————. (1921). *Psychological Types. Coll. Wks.* 6.

————. (1912). *Symbols of Transformation. Coll. Wks.* 5.

————. (1939). "The Concept of the Collective Unconscious." *Coll. Wks.* 9, 1.

————. (1943). "The Gifted Child." *Coll. Wks.* 17.

————. (1951). "The Psychology of the Child Archetype." *Coll. Wks.* 9, 1.

————. (1946). "The Psychology of the Transference." *Coll. Wks.* 16.

————. (1951). "The Shadow." *Coll. Wks.* 9, 2.

————. (1909). "The Significance of the Father in the Destiny of the Individual." *Coll. Wks.* 4.

————. (1930-31). "The Stages of Life." *Coll. Wks.* 8.

————. (1913). "The Theory of Psychoanalysis." *Coll. Wks.* 4..

Klein, M. (1959). "The Sexual Development of the Girl." In *Psychoanalysis of Children.* London: The Hogarth Press.

Lambert, K. (1981). *Analysis, Repair and Individuation.* L.A.P. London: H. Karnac Books.

Lichtenberg, J. (1983). *Psychoanalysis and Infant Research.* Hillsdale, NJ: The Analytic Press.

MacDougall, J. (1986). *The Theater of the Mind: Illusion and Truth on the Psychoanalytic Stage.* London: Free Association.

Miller, S. (1986). *The Experience of Shame.* London: The Analytic Press.

Neumann, E. (1956). *The Origins and History of Consciousness.* Princeton: Princeton University Press.

Ogden, T. (1986). *The Matrix of the Mind.* New York: Jason Aronson.

Peterson, G. (1978) "Some Determinants of Maternal Attachment." In *American Journal of Psychiatry,* 135: 168-173.

Piaget, J. (1937/54). *The Construction of Reality in Children.* New York: Basic Books.

Piontelli, S. (1987). *International Journal of Psychoanalysis* 68: 453.

Prechtel, Heinz. Personal communication with the author.

Proner, B. (1983). "Attacks on Analysis." The *Journal of Analytical Psychology,* 28, 3.

Stein, L. (1967). "Introducing Not-self." *The Journal of Analytical Psychology,* 12, 2.

Strauss, Ruth (1964). "The Archetype of Separation." *International Congress of Analytical Psychology.* Basel: Schrager.

Tate-Davidson, D. (1956). "On Ego Development." *The Journal of Analytical Psychology,* 3, 2.

Tustin, F. (1986). *Autistic Barriers in Neurotic Patients.* London: H. Karnac Books.

Tustin, F. (1981). *Autistic States in Children.* London: Routledge & Kegan Paul.

Winnicot, D.W. (1971). *Playing and Reality.* London: Pelican Books.

Index

SIGO PRESS

SIGO PRESS publishes books in psychology
which continue the work of C.G. Jung, the great
Swiss psychoanalyst and founder of analytical
psychology. Each season SIGO brings out a small
but distinctive list of titles intended to make a
lasting contribution to psychology and human
thought. These books are invaluable reading for
Jungians, psychologists, students and scholars
and provide enrichment and insight to general
readers as well. In the Jungian Classics Series,
well-known Jungian works are brought back into
print in popular editions.

Other Titles from Sigo Press

The Unholy Bible *by June Singer*
$32.00 cloth, $15.95 paper

Emotional Child Abuse *by Joel Covitz*
$24.95 cloth, $13.95 paper

Dreams of a Woman *by Shelia Moon*
$27.50 cloth, $13.95 paper

Androgyny *by June Singer*
$24.95 cloth, $14.95 paper

The Dream-The Vision of the Night *by Max Zeller*
$21.95 cloth, $14.95 paper

Sandplay Studies *by Bradway et al.*
$35.00 cloth, $18.95 paper

Symbols Come Alive in the Sand *by Evelyn Dundas*
$27.50 cloth, $14.95 paper

Inner World of Childhood *by Frances G. Wickes*
$27.50 cloth, $14.95 paper

Inner World of Man *by Frances G. Wickes*
$27.50 cloth, $14.95 paper

Inner World of Choice *by Frances G. Wickes*
$27.50 cloth, $14.95 paper

*Available from SIGO PRESS, 25 New Chardon Street, #8748A,
Boston, Massachusetts, 02114. tel. (508) 526-7064*

*In England: Element Books. Ltd., Longmead, Shaftesbury, Dorset.
SP7 8PL. tel. (0747) 51339, Shaftesbury.*